FORESTS
OF THE NIGHT

July 8, 1999

To my good

friend and colleague —

Niles

FORESTS
OF THE NIGHT

The Fear of God
in Early Hasidic Thought

NILES ELLIOT GOLDSTEIN

JASON ARONSON INC.
Northvale, New Jersey
London

This book was set in 12 pt. Garamond by Alpha Graphics of Pittsfield, N.H.

Manufactured in the United States of America. Jason Aronson Inc. offers books and cassettes. For information and catalog write to Jason Aronson Inc., 230 Livingston Street, Northvale, New Jersey 07647.

For my mother and father

Contents

Tyger Tyger burning bright,
In the forests of the night:
What immortal hand or eye,
Dare frame thy fearful symmetry?

William Blake, "The Tyger"

Preface

This book has its roots in personal experience. Were it not for my own brushes with the world of the spirit— some of which took place in forests, some on mountaintops—I very much doubt I would ever have considered becoming a rabbi, let alone felt compelled to critically explore such fearful and formative encounters. I thank God for these and other gifts of grace that continue to shape my life.

When I first heard the voices of Yaakov Yosef and Dov Baer, two of the most important and pivotal figures in the hasidic movement, they sounded to me like blasts from a shofar. In this time of spiritual disillusionment, when so many of us are alienated from our houses of worship and so much of what passes for "spirituality" is both faddish and facile, the words of these eighteenth-century rabbis broke through the vacuum and served as food for my soul.

For them, the fear of God is the cornerstone of the inner life. It is not a posture, but a spiritual necessity.

Their ruminations on the phenomenon of fear, as it applies to a Jew's relationship with God, are as passionate as they are complex. This book strives to examine and compare the views of the two men, paying close attention to the kabbalistic context from which their views emerged, as well as the forks and departures they were forced to make along their own mystical paths.

This book was first written as my rabbinical thesis at the Hebrew Union College-Jewish Institute of Religion. I am grateful to Elliot Wolfson, my principal advisor on this project, whose critical eye and breadth of knowledge on matters mystical were invaluable. I am also indebted to Eugene Borowitz, whose demand for intellectual honesty has been as constant as it has been intense. I thank my editor, Arthur Kurzweil, without whose support this material might not have reached a wider audience. In addition, Michael Signer, Steven Golden, Norman Cohen, and Lawrence Raphael have helped me in more ephemeral but still significant ways.

And, of course, I owe a special debt of gratitude to the rest of the Four Horsemen: Andrew Bachman, Daniel Bronstein, and Joshua Saltzman. Their friendship has been almost alchemic, transforming tears into laughter and the profane into the sacred. Their presence will be with me for years to come.

Brooklyn, New York   Niles Elliot Goldstein
Tu B'shvat 5756

Introduction

The fear of God has been a fundamental Jewish motif
for nearly three thousand years. As one might suspect,
its importance to the religious life reached full flower
in more esoteric and pietistic circles, where internality
tended to be emphasized at least as strongly as external behavior. Yet the concept was never absent from
the normative Jewish tradition: he who possessed the
"fear of God" was depicted as a model Jew, a man of
faith and high ethical principles. The idea, however,
remained amorphous for hundreds of years; it seemed
to designate certain *general* religious qualities, but its
precise meaning was never systematically explored until
the Middle Ages.

The fear of God as a Jewish notion has roots as
far back as the book of Genesis. In the Akedah story,
Abraham is called a *yerei Elohim* (Gen. 22:12), or "fearer
of God." In this context, as Kierkegaard has shown us,[1]
yirah has less to do with ethicality than with faith and
submission. Louis Jacobs notes,[2] however, that the fear

1

of God also seems "to express an especially intense relationship with God, especially as realized in terms of high ethical conduct." Job, for instance, is described as "perfect and upright, and one who feared God, and turned away from evil" (Job 1:1).

The Bible suggests elsewhere that the fear of God is of critical import for a life of happiness and virtue (see Ps. 112:1 and Prov. 19:23). The notion of *yirah* is also connected to specific interpersonal relations (see Lev. 19:14, 19:32, 25:17, and 25:36). The fear of God finds yet another association with regard to the life of the mind, as in "The fear of the Lord is the beginning of wisdom" (Ps. 111:10), and "The fear of the Lord is the beginning of knowledge" (Prov. 1:7).

In rabbinic literature, the fear of God is generally called *yirat shamayim* (as opposed to *yirat Elohim* or *yirat Adonai*), yet its precise meaning remains unclear. In this genre, the fear of God is generally linked to the love of God, and discussions on the topic tend to focus on the interrelationship between these two attitudes/ responses toward God (see M. Avot 1:3, BT Sotah 31a, and Tos. Sotah 6:1). In early medieval thought, religious fear is subdivided into two discrete types: the fear of punishment (*yirat ha-onesh*) and the fear of God's majesty (*yirat ha-rommemut*). This distinction will cata- lyze a wide range of speculation on the subject for the next several centuries.

In *Duties of the Heart*, Bakhya ibn Pakudah claims that only the latter, higher form of fear can lead to— and is the prerequisite for—the love of God. The fear of punishment, while important for right conduct, is a fear of a far lower order and without merit in terms of one's internal religious quality.[3] We shall examine the view of Maimonides later in this book. Suffice it to note here that he, too, endorses Bakhya's hierarchy of value and denigrates the fear of punishment as an improper way of serving God. The fear of God, though important, gains its value only because it stimulates religious observance and leads to the higher love of God, which, for him, is intellectual perfection.[4]

Joseph Albo writes in *Sefer ha-Ikkarim* that the fear of punishment, while not meritorious, is a necessary condition for the attainment of the fear of God's majesty. The former kind of fear, he comments, subdues man's physical nature, while the latter type, better understood as awe, is reason's natural response to the unveiling of the religious truth embedded within him. Unlike his predecessors, Albo argues that the fear of God, rather than the love of God, is the conduit to intellectual perfection.[5] Other medieval thinkers, particularly Judah the Hasid, focus almost exclusively on the pietistic and ethical issues surrounding the concept of *yirah*. In this context, fear is treated as an attitude that gives the pietist the strength to overcome his worldly desires, as well as the proof of his faith.[6]

Elijah de Vidas and Judah Loew offer two spiritualist approaches to the notion of religious fear. De Vidas devotes the first fifteen chapters of *Reshit Hokhmah* to theosophical reflections on fear and sin. In the kabbalistic context, the fear of punishment (for sin), far from being the mere fear of self-harm, becomes instead the fear of causing a "flaw" in the divine cosmos. Though it is not as lofty as *yirat ha-rommemut*, it is not at all denigrated by de Vidas.[7] Loew views the higher fear as the prerequisite for adhesion with God; without its power to cause self-abnegation, one cannot reach the level of spiritual love, which is the last step in the ascent to divine communion.[8]

Until the beginning of the hasidic period (near the middle of the eighteenth century), discussions on the fear of God generally approached the topic from ethical, pietistic, or philosophical vantage points. Though there were some exceptions—most notably in more mystical circles—it is only after the emergence of hasidism that we find a sophisticated and well-developed *phenomenological* analysis of the fear of God. While mooring themselves in the kabbalistic hermeneutics they inherited, the early hasidic mystics go beyond theosophical speculation and examine the fear of God as it relates to *unio mystica*—the actual encounter with divinity. The hasidic innovations are most clearly seen in their descriptions of the various spiritual phenomena which accompany such an encounter.

In terms of modern scholarship on the subject of the fear of God, we find a virtual terra incognita. I have not been able to find even a single monograph (in English) on the topic. What does exist is careful in its analysis but woefully inadequate in its depth and scope. In *God in Search of Man: A Philosophy of Judaism* (1955), Abraham Joshua Heschel devotes barely six pages to the concept of *yirah* in Jewish thought. Louis Jacobs, in *A Jewish Theology* (1973), perhaps the best critical study on religious fear, contributes a chapter on this topic. The most recent addition to this area is an essay on *yirah* by Byron Sherwin in *Contemporary Jewish Religious Thought* (1988). Since all of these pieces are surveys, they offer little comprehensive insight into the notion of *yirah* as it relates either to individual thinkers or to particular genres.

With regard to the fear of God in hasidic thought specifically, the situation is no better. As Jacobs himself notes, there is no lack of critical scholarship on the practical aspects of hasidism, nor on its history, sociology, tales, or legends; yet "little has been done to examine hasidic thought in a systematic way."[9] (The major exceptions, such as Gershom Scholem, Rivka Schatz-Uffenheimer, and Joseph Weiss, shall be cited throughout this book.) Even the work that has been done in hasidic thought has failed to confront the fear of God as a topic in its own right.

Why has there been such a vacuum in research? I would argue that there have been two fundamental stumbling blocks to scholarly advancement on this subject: methodological difficulties and the modern mindset. Since the hasidic masters used the homily (*derashah*) as their primary mode of transmission, the presentation of their ideas is far from systematic: their language of discourse is a complex mosaic of rabbinic Hebrew, Aramaic, and obscure kabbalistic terminology; the works themselves are poorly organized; it is hard to determine the authenticity of teachings attributed to particular masters; there are alternative manuscripts to many of the texts, complicating efforts to trace citations.

Classical Judaic scholars (with the exception of Hillel Zeitlin) treated the hasidic mind with great disdain. Even in the absence of this bias, however, the influence of modern rationalism made later scholars reluctant to try to penetrate the "primitivity" of hasidism's mystical jargon and imagery. I contend that this selfsame rationalism prevented scholars from exploring the theological significance of the fear of God. Moderns were simply not comfortable with an idea such as religious fear, which must have seemed to them like a wild animal: naked, untamable, and beyond intellectualization. Further, Martin Buber's impact on Jewish theology should not be overlooked. By positing love as the *ex-*

clusive response to the I-Thou encounter, Buber leaves no room for its spiritual sibling, fear. This contortion of the love/fear dialectic has influenced much of Jewish thought to this day.

Though the fear of God has always been a key concept in Jewish thought, it seems to have reached its highest degree of sophistication and development in the phenomenology of hasidism. In addition to the above methodological problems, a study on a motif such as *yirah* must also face the problem of focus. I have chosen to compare two of hasidism's first and most important masters: R. Yaakov Yosef of Polonnoye and R. Dov Baer of Mezeritch. Each thinker presents a starkly different view of religious fear and demonstrates that even in the first generation after the Baal Shem Tov there existed at least the seeds of widely divergent branches within the hasidic movement.

I

The Toledot: Yaakov Yosef Ha-Kohen of Polonnoye

Yaakov Yosef (d. 1782) was the first theoretician of the nascent hasidic movement. As one of the initial disciples of Israel ben Eliezer, or the Baal Shem Tov, it was Yaakov Yosef who wrote down and expounded the teachings of his master, as Plato voiced the words of Socrates. He came to hasidism later in life, as a convert to it, having had at first opposed the radicalism of these "new" ideas.[1] Yet he was to become one of its most zealous proponents and a fierce critic of the rabbinic leadership of his time. As a result of his positions, Yaakov Yosef spent much of his life moving from one community to another.

Yaakov Yosef's writings are full of references to the Zohar and pietistic texts, though he also makes wide use of Jewish legal material, such as the medieval codes. His first and principal work (and the name by which he was to become known) was *Toledot Yaakov Yosef* (Koretz, 1780), a collection of homilies on the Torah, the "words which I heard from my master," the Baal Shem Tov. His other books are *Ben Porat Yosef* (Koretz, 1781), a group of sermons based primarily on Genesis; *Zafnat Paneah* (Koretz, 1782), a commentary on the book of Exodus; and *Ketonet Passim* (Lemberg, 1866), a commentary on Leviticus and Numbers published long after his death.

In order to discover Yaakov Yosef's theological views, it is necessary to examine these homiletical writings and extrapolate from them his approaches to particular religious concepts such as the fear of God. As the result of methodological necessity, our study does not include the legends and tales *about* Yaakov Yosef, since most (if not all) of them are hagiographic works, and thus unreliable as texts through which we may come to understand his thought. The systematization of a body of *un*systematic literature is a difficult task, but it is to this task that our research is devoted.

The Baal Shem Tov died in 1760, and it is well known that Yaakov Yosef lost the struggle to be his successor, and for gaining his disciples, to the younger Dov Baer. What may not be as clear, however, is just how different were the spiritual systems of these two seminal thinkers. An examination of their views on the fear of God provides us with insight into this difference. In chapter one, we focus on Yaakov Yosef's idea of the zaddik and how it relates to the attainment of the fear of God. Chapter two delineates the various typologies of religious fear present in his system. Chapter three discusses how these discrete orders of fear interact with one another, and chapter four analyzes the purpose behind, and the phenomenological effects of, the fear of God.

1

The Zaddik and Mediation

Yaakov Yosef's notion of the zaddik is central to a full understanding of his idea of the fear of God (or, for that matter, any other attribute or modality which serves to connect the human with the divine). As our author writes, "It is only possible to join together two opposites through a third force."[1] The interplay, on any level, of the temporal with the eternal, of the finite with infinity, necessitates the mediation of some outside element. That element is the zaddik.

The *Toledot* itself is very much concerned with this issue. As the first published work on hasidism, it is used by Yaakov Yosef as a forum by which he expounds his concept of mediation and sets the tone for much of the later literature on the subject of the zaddik. (This latter material will serve to express the transformation—or denigration—of hasidism into zaddikism.) Hasidism's founder, the Baal Shem Tov, viewed himself as the medium through which the masses would tap into the new religious consciousness; he considered himself a teacher of "the fear of heaven."[2]

Since it is the stated purpose of the *Toledot* to explain and discuss each of the Torah's 613 commandments,[3] it will be critical, with regard to the notion of the fear of God, to examine Yaakov Yosef's homilies on the chapter where the commandment to fear God first appears. In his section on "Ekev," in response to the verse, "Thou shalt fear the Lord thy God,"[4] Yaakov Yosef writes:

> The author of *Halakhot Gedolot* [an eighth-century legal code of disputed authorship] considers the fear of scholars one of the positive commandments, since the Talmud interprets "Thou shalt fear the Lord thy God" to include scholars (BT Baba Kamma 41b). However, [in the *Mishneh Torah*] Maimonides writes, "There is no basis for this [claim]." Nahmanides supports the view of the author of *Halakhot Gedolot*, while our great teacher Rabbi Isaac de Leon supports the view of Maimonides.[5]

The debate here centers on the issue of whether or not the biblical commandment to fear God necessitates the additional injunction to fear scholars. The normative phrase for scholar is *talmid hakham*, which Yaakov Yosef uses throughout his literary corpus as a generic term for the zaddik.[6] As we will see, it is this notion of the zaddik that our author develops and uses to express the phenomenon of mediation, without which true fear of God would be impossible.

On the legal issue, Yaakov Yosef sides with Maimonides and de Leon, who argue that the fear of God encompasses the fear of scholars and that therefore no additional commandment is needed. He writes: "With regard to the matter of fear: there is no need for a special commandment to fear scholars, since [this commandment] is included in [the commandment to] fear God."[7] The establishment of a connection between "God" and "scholars" is clear; Yaakov Yosef now turns to the utilization of such a linkage. He asserts that

> we learn from many sources another specific matter with regard to the fear of scholars, the love of scholars, and, as it is written, "to him shalt thou cleave" [Deu. 10:20]—[that is,] cleave to scholars [BT Ketubot 111b]. How will the masses find the way, so that they may cleave to God, may He be blessed? And how will they fear Him? The author of *Halakhot Gedolot* discovered a medium, and this is the scholar: [it is] through him [that] one is able to enter the levels mentioned above, though without him this is impossible. . . .[8]

This passage is representative of Yaakov Yosef's views on our topic in a number of ways. Of immediate import is his grouping together of three central and discrete hasidic motifs: fear, love, and adhesion, or *devekut*. (We will return to this unusual merger in the next chapter.)

Here, these phenomena relate primarily to the scholar, the zaddik. Just as the Talmud extends the fear of God to also encompass scholars, so too does it extend the notion of adhesion to God. Significantly, both imperatives—to fear God and to cleave to God—appear in the selfsame verse. Our author's concern is with the *mechanism* through which the "masses" will be able to satisfy these difficult commands. As we mentioned at the outset, Yaakov Yosef thinks that a union of opposites is only possible through their interaction with a third force. For Yaakov Yosef, that third force, or medium, is the zaddik. It is only through the ontic interplay of the masses with the zaddik that the most profound spiritual levels become accessible to them. While the author of *Halakhot Gedolot* considers it a commandment to fear scholars as well as God, Yaakov Yosef explodes this principle and transforms the zaddik into a *devar memutza*, a mediator between the human and the divine.[9] In this sense, Yaakov Yosef belongs to both camps of the earlier argument: though he rejects the need for an extra commandment to fear scholars, he accepts the implicit idea that the zaddik does indeed have a distinct and critical function which cannot be subsumed under a general rubric related to God.[10]

It should be clear that, for the masses, the fear of God must be mediated through the fear of the zaddik. Whatever this notion means, its *direct* experience is not possible for the average man. There are two consequences of such a position, both of which are consistent with the elitist/populist tension in most of Yaakov Yosef's writings. On one hand, without the ontological presence of the zaddik, individual spiritual growth can never rise above its most mundane levels. On the other hand, *anyone*, with the zaddik's mediation, can transcend himself and climb to the highest rungs of the Godhead.

Let us now examine the actual dynamic of this spiritual ascent. Yaakov Yosef writes that

> . . . [it is] through humility [that one] comes to fear. Yet although the fear and terror from [being in the presence of] a flesh and blood king comes of itself through [merely] seeing him . . . it is not the case with regard to God, may He be blessed. The foundation of fear [in this case derives] from intellectual vision, which is an aspect of knowledge, and reflection on the greatness

of God's majesty, may He be blessed. With regard to
the masses, those who are far from knowledge and
reflection, it seems to me that they need to fear the
scholars, whose words they can hear. [The scholars] will
awaken their hearts until the fear and the terror of
God's glory, may He be blessed, will likewise come to
them—and this too depends on humility. . . .[11]

One of the key motifs present in this passage is that
of humility, of the awareness of one's own insignificance
in the face of that which is greater. While the presence
of a real-life king—which is concrete and tangible—is
in itself sufficient to elicit fear from one of his subjects,
the reality of God—which is ephemeral and ineffable—
is not. The fear of God, claims Yaakov Yosef, has its
roots in the intellect, and, as such, is beyond the ken of
the minds of the masses. One cannot be humbled before
that which one cannot understand and therefore cannot
experience. In this way, the masses must first fear the
zaddik, whose "words" are (or palpability is) within their
grasp. It is the humility they feel before the zaddik that
will serve as the stage from which to advance to the
higher humility, and higher fear, of God.

This spiritual elevation must be a gradual one. The
masses must first of all be "awakened" from their slumber, a slumber which prevents them from attaining
any of the more metaphysical attributes. While contact
with a corporeal king is enough to cause the automatic
response of fear and trembling, contact with a spiritual
king ("the King, the Lord of Hosts"[12]) can only take place
through the mediation of the zaddik, and thus can only
be indirect. Mediation is even necessary for the zaddik
himself: though he alone is capable of achieving the
"intellectual vision" of God, that insight must forever

remain the buffer between his finitude and God's infinity. For, as Yaakov Yosef cautions his reader, "No man shall see me, and live."[13]

The notion that the fear of God should extend to the fear of scholars is introduced by Rabbi Akiba in the Babylonian Talmud (Baba Kamma 41b). Yaakov Yosef presents a midrash to explain how he came to such an interpretation:

> When [Rabbi Akiba] was an ignorant man, he hated scholars, and he was far from the fear of God, may He be blessed. But when he [himself] became a scholar, he feared the rabbis, and drew close to the fear of God, may He be blessed, as well. Thus he interpreted "[Fear] God" (Deu. 10:20) to include scholars, because the fear of scholars brings one to the fear of God, may He be blessed.[14]

Yaakov Yosef views Rabbi Akiba's metamorphosis from an ignoramus into a *talmid hakham* as a transformation not only of intellect, but also of inner attitude. There is a direct correlation between the "fear" one feels toward great scholars and the fear one feels toward God. For the man who lacks the proper reverence for those greater than himself, the awe for "that than which a greater cannot be thought" (to quote from Anselm's *Proslogion*) is a remote possibility. Yaakov Yosef goes on to posit that the generation of the Exodus had, in fact, the proper disposition:

> When Israel was in the desert, they had the fear of scholars, as it is written, ". . . and they were afraid to come near him" [Ex. 34:30]. If this is the case, then they easily acquired the fear of God as well. From this we can understand [the talmudic statement] "Nothing with

regard to Moses was a small matter" [BT Berakhot 33b].
It means to say, since [Israel] had fear because of Moses,
they merited the fear of scholars. If so, it was a small
matter for them to merit the fear of God as well. Understand this.[15]

Israel's fear of Moses is translated into the fear of scholars, which in turn brings them to the fear of God. This
passage is used to complement the preceding one. It is
a small step to reach the fear of God when one already
possesses the preparatory fear of scholars. And though
the achievement of this level seems almost too easy for
Israel to acquire, it is only easy because their fear of
Moses has *already* brought them to a great spiritual
height. Lest one think that the fear of God is a small
matter, Yaakov Yosef makes clear just the opposite: its
attainment is simple only in a relative sense—after one
has reached the point of its actual threshold.

The introduction of Moses in the previous text is
not accidental. As we shall see, Moses becomes, for
Yaakov Yosef, the very paradigm for his notion of the
zaddik—the intermediary through which Israel is able
to achieve the highest levels of relationship with God.
Our author asserts this notion in the clearest terms: ". . .
he who believes in and cleaves to the Shepherd of Israel
[Moses] will, from this, cleave to God."[16] It seems mediation, via Moses/the zaddik, is as reliable as it is necessary. Yaakov Yosef contends

 . . . that those who have faith in Moses, who is connected to the Root, will have faith in God . . . since the
 public leader must, for the sake of heaven, direct the
 people practically and spiritually—not with deeds and
 words alone, . . . but also in thought, for he joins himself to God, may He be blessed, and afterwards tries to

join himself with the people of his generation, to elevate them and make them cleave with God, may He
be blessed. . . . This is the meaning of the phrase, "When
one has faith in a shepherd of Israel, it is as if he has
faith in God [Himself], may He be blessed,"[17] for the
former is the means to the latter. . . . It is through be-
lieving in Moses that [Israel] was made to cleave with
God.[18]

Moses, unlike other human beings, is joined to
God—the "Root." He is the critical link in the great chain
of being, the connective tissue between humanity and
divinity. To have faith in Moses is, through association,
to have faith in God. Moses, like all later zaddikim, must
serve as the guide for his people, the shepherd who will
direct their external as well as internal behavior. It is
via this *devekut*, or adhesion, of the zaddik to his people
that he is able to elevate them so that they, too, may
adhere to their God. For the generation of the Exodus,
it was through this dynamic that adhesion with God
became possible.

The consequences of such a view are radical: the
Exodus from slavery in Egypt thus becomes the work
of Moses, and not God. Yaakov Yosef writes:

All this [the liberation from Egypt and the later achievement of the fear of God] was made possible via Moses,
who was the intermediary [between Israel and God],
. . . and who opened for them the channel to the highest
fear, which comes from [the sefirah] *binah*. Hence it is
written, "And Moses took the bones of Joseph with him"
[Ex. 13:19]—which means to say, he took with him the
nature and essence[19] of Joseph, for [it was] through
external fear that Joseph was aroused to internal fear,
and recognized that this was God's will, may He be
blessed.[20]

Yaakov Yosef introduces in this passage a new word related to the phenomenon of mediation: *tzinor*, or channel. Moses, the prototypical zaddik, does more than merely serve as the bridge between two planes of being; he actually has the power to open the "channel" into the supernal world. Rather than passively allowing for the interplay of the human with the divine, Moses/the zaddik actively effects a rupture in the metaphysical dam: he brings about the irruption of heaven down to earth—in this case, the *fear* of heaven. (We shall examine the above notions of fear in the following chapter.) Joseph's bones provide the embodiment of the idea of channeling. Just as Joseph was able to break through the fears of this world and attain the fear of heaven, so Moses, who "carries" with him Joseph's ability, brings to his own people access to this highest degree of fear.

It is through the sheer physicality of Moses that communion with God, and with the divine influx, becomes a possibility for Israel. After God sends poisonous serpents against Israel as punishment for their insubordination, the people plead with Moses to intercede on their behalf, to ask God for relief from their misery. God responds to Moses: "Make thee a venomous serpent, and set it upon a pole: and it shall come to pass, that every one that is bitten, when he looks upon it, shall live" (Num. 21:8). Yaakov Yosef writes:

> The meaning of "every one that is bitten" is external fear: if one [who is bitten] looks up and is brought via [the serpent] to internal fear—which is the submission of one's heart to his Father in heaven—he will be healed and freed from external fear. All this is due to the hand of Moses, who is the intermediary, and who elevates Israel to his own level, which is internal fear. Understand this.[21]

In this passage, as in the preceding one, Moses is given the full credit for Israel's ultimate triumph over hardship. Though it is God who directs the drama and issues the commands, it is Moses who carries Joseph's bones into the desert and Moses who erects the serpent of brass to heal his people. Moses/the zaddik is the visible representation of God's hand, but he is more than that: he is the workhorse who bears the yoke of his people's trials and aspirations. His mere presence offers hope and makes redemption a possibility. Just as the vision of the serpent serves to connect its witness with his God, so does the life of the zaddik help his community to free itself from the terrors of this world—and to bring it with him to the fear of God.

2

Typologies of Fear

In the previous chapter we discussed Yaakov Yosef's notion of mediation as it relates to the phenomenon of the fear of God. Let us now turn to an analysis of this fear itself. As we have already seen, the concept is neither uniform nor clear: there are several different types of religious fear, each with its own particular object and/or function. The fear of zaddikim, for instance, is (for the masses) the prerequisite for the fear of God. Yet for our author, as for the many Jewish writers before him,[1] an examination of the fear of God is almost impossible without at least a partial treatment of its spiritual sibling, the love of God. These two religious attributes have not always been described with consistent or clear distinctions and have sometimes (seemingly) been used interchangeably. In our discussion of the fear of God that follows, we will examine the love of God only as it relates to our primary interest.

Yaakov Yosef claims that these attributes permeate all modes of existence:

I have learned from the mouths of sages and writers a great thing which is found in the world, and this is the matter of fear and love, which is found in all the worlds —[the worlds of] emanation, creation, formation, and making—and in all the [spiritual] levels. . . . This begins from the smallest of creatures: for the mouse fears the cat, and the cat fears the dog, and thus the kid the wolf, and the wolf the lion, and [so on with] the rest of the predatory animals. Likewise with birds and with human beings: the weaker fears the stronger. And the fear of a kingship is felt by all human beings, [and so on] until the highest point, which is the Root of every fear, as it is written: ". . . what does the Lord thy God require of thee, but to fear the Lord thy God . . ." [Deu. 10:12].[2]

In this passage Yaakov Yosef posits the notion that fear inheres in the entire hierarchy of being and is intimately connected with the phenomena of relationship and power. What is unclear, however, is whether this fear differs only in its object (e.g., a cat as opposed to God), or in *kind*. Does the lesser being, of necessity, fear its superior? Does the fear of God involve a qualitative, or merely a quantitative, difference? Our author will address this issue later in his writings. Of immediate note, however, is the fact that Yaakov Yosef views the fear of God as the terminus for and root of all other fears. This point will be taken up in chapter four.

A clear division of religious fear into distinct categories appears in an interpetation of a line from the Mishnah:

"Antigonos of Sokho received [the tradition] from Simon the Just. He used to say: Be not like slaves who serve their master for the sake of receiving a reward; rather, be like slaves who serve their master without the expectation of a reward—and let the fear of heaven be upon you" [Avot 1:3]. This means that one should fear due to the majesty and greatness of God, may He be blessed, and not because of [the threat of] punishment. For one who refrains from sinning out of [the fear of] punishment is not a God-fearer; it is only himself whom he fears.[3]

The line to which Yaakov Yosef is responding here most probably contains one of the earliest postbiblical usages of the phrase "fear of heaven," or, in later manifestations, the "fear of God."[4] Two types of fear are distilled from it: the fear of punishment and the fear of God's majesty. He who fears God only because of the threat of punishment is like the slave who serves his master only for the sake of a reward. The object of this kind of submission is either the absence of some punishment or the promise of some reward. In neither scenario is the object of service God/the master himself. Yaakov Yosef denigrates this kind of fear: a fear with an inferior object is a fear of inferior worth. He does not claim that he who resists sin cannot be a God-fearer, but he does argue that if that resistance is based upon an unworthy motivation (the fear of punishment), its value is negated. This type of person has no one but himself as his ultimate concern and motivation. For Yaakov Yosef, this kind of fear seems to border on idolatry.

True service of a master/God involves no such external motivations. He who fears God for His own sake is like the slave who serves his master without the expectation of (or even desire for) a reward. It is the sheer force of God's majesty and greatness that compels this type of fear, just as it is only the wish to serve his master which motivates the slave. Rather than being rooted in negativity, these responses have *positive* moorings. In these situations, the object of submission is solely God/

the master; there are no secondary, or extrinsic, motivations for behavior. The Mishnah seems to connect this kind of service with the fear of heaven, as does Yaakov Yosef: the threat of punishment and the promise of reward play no role in his conception of the fear of God. (From his comparison of the dynamic of master/slave with that of God/man, it should be clear that the lines between love and fear as the bases for motivation seem to coalesce. This idea of merger will prove to be a key point in Yaakov Yosef's spiritual system.)

Our author quotes from Maimonides in an effort to clarify the mechanism by which one may come to achieve these higher levels of relationship to God:

> It is a commandment to love and to fear the glorious and awesome God, as it is written, "And thou shalt love the Lord thy God," [Deu. 6:5] and "thou shalt fear the Lord thy God" [Deu. 6:13]. But what is the path to love and to fear Him? When one reflects on His wondrous deeds and creatures . . . one is immediately [filled with] love [for God]. . . . And when one contemplates these things themselves, one immediately trembles . . . and grows fearful, for he becomes conscious [of the fact] that he is a tiny and lowly creature, with meager knowledge compared to [He who possesses] perfect knowledge.[5]

The "path" toward the love and fear of God is, for Maimonides, a cognitive one. It is in the intellectual apprehension of God's omnipotence—which stems from one's reflection on the material world, the world "out there"—that one becomes filled with a sense of love for the world's Creator. When one contemplates these things *themselves*, however—when one thinks about their ontic reality, rather than God's creative power—

one is gripped by fear and trembling. It is the realization of one's existential situation, one's finitude in the face of the infinite, that results in fear. The distinctions are profound: love relates to epistemic awareness, while fear is the response to a more primitive existential/ontological consciousness. In the philosophical system of Maimonides, knowledge of the former sort is clearly favored.

Maimonides elsewhere comments on the order of precedence for these two religious responses. He writes, "Love never precedes, but only follows, fear."[6] Yaakov Yosef supports this claim. He argues that both reason and Scripture affirm the order of this sequence—fear must always precede love. Using as a proof-text the verse "The fear of the Lord is the beginning of wisdom" (Ps. 111:10), Yaakov Yosef states: "Fear is the portal and gate through which one enters [in order to] reach the level of love."[7] From these comments, Yaakov Yosef quite clearly holds the position that the fear of God is subsidiary to and the prerequisite of the love of God.

Our author breaks down these phenomena into lower and higher orders, thus creating four basic typologies:

> There are two types of fear and two types of love. . . . This is the consequence [of the fact] that fear is situated in *malkhut* and love is situated in *ze'ir anpin* [the sefirot above *malkhut* and below *keter*] while internal fear is located in *hokhmah* and internal love in *binah*, as is known. The fear of *malkhut* is *din* . . . while the love of *ze'ir anpin* is the love of reward. If this is the case, then [this kind of love] is contingent on the thing that one loves, in that one does not [want to] lose the benefit from it; if it is lost, then the love departs from him. Likewise with regard to the fear [of *malkhut*]: if

one who fears death and affliction becomes tormented
and kills himself, he no longer fears them—which is
not the case with regard to internal fear and love. There
is another consequence: in a place where there is fear,
which is *din*, there cannot be love, which is *hesed*. This
is not the case with regard to internal fear and love,
since they derive from God's majesty and are one: [the
supernal] father and mother, "firm friends who never
separate" [Zohar III:4a]. There is a third consequence,
in that the fear of *malkhut* precedes the love of *ze'ir
anpin*, which is not the case with internal love and fear,
where the love in *binah* precedes the fear in *hokhmah*.[8]

Yaakov Yosef posits three important consequences
that result from this quartet of religious responses.
Whereas the two highest, or "internal," forms of fear and
love are to be found near the summit of the sefirotic
ladder (*hokhmah* and *binah*), the two lower forms reside
at the center and bottom (*ze'ir anpin* and *malkhut*). Fear
at the level of *malkhut*—which serves as the gateway
to the sefirot—is associated with the attribute of *din*,
the left side of the kabbalistic schema. Love, at this lesser
level, is connected with *ze'ir anpin*: the second and
lower "divine face."[9] (The higher/internal forms of
fear and love, on the other hand, are the aspects, or
partzufim, of *abbah* and *immah*, or the supernal father
and mother, which are just below *arikh anpin*, the highest "divine face.") The lower order of love has, as its
object of concern, the acquisition of reward or benefit.
If that object is beyond one's grasp, or if it is lost, then
the love itself loses its footing and vanishes. In a similar way, the lower order of fear dissipates once its object of concern is no longer pertinent. These responses
are not "pure," but rather *contingent*, responses—without their objects they do not and cannot exist.

There is a second consequence of this theosophical dynamic: the problem of the coexistence of opposites. With regard to the lower forms of fear and love, this kind of cohabitation is, in principle, impossible. As we have noted above, the lower types of fear and love (which are part of *ze'ir anpin*) are associated, respectively, with the attributes of *din* and *hesed*. The former attribute is part of the left, feminine side of the sefirotic tree, while the latter belongs to the right, masculine side. For Yaakov Yosef, any potential relationship between the two is negated due to their mutual exclusivity. Where there is fear, there cannot be love, and where there is love, there cannot be fear. Since these responses are contingent ones, each one's object of concern is the critical and ultimate referent—and one cannot both fear *and* love the same object simultaneously.

The opposite is the case with regard to the higher forms of fear and love, which are "internal," i.e., lack any extrinsic concern or contingency. Here, the dual religious responses stem from the *arikh anpin*—the higher divine configuration. They are associated with *binah* (love) and *hokhmah* (fear), which rest below, and emanate from, the first and greatest sefirah, *keter*. Yaakov Yosef argues that internal love and fear derive from God's "majesty" (*rommemut*), which he apparently connects with *keter*. These two responses are thus viewed as having no real "object of concern," in that God's majesty offers neither benefit nor detriment: it is the source not of motivation, but of immediate and spontaneous reaction. With the notion of any contingency removed, internal fear and love are indeed able to co-exist; they become, in the zoharic system, the supernal father and mother, out of which issue all of the lower sefirot.

The third and final consequence of these higher and lower orders relates both to sequence and stature. While in his preceding comments on the passage from Maimonides our author places fear before and subsidiary to love, we see here that this holds only with regard to the lower levels of these responses—the fear of *malkhut* clearly precedes and is below the love of *ze'ir anpin*. At the higher levels, however, the structure is reversed: it is love (in *binah*) which precedes and is subordinate to fear (in *hokhmah*).[10] This shift occurs for a specific reason. Though its position and priority may differ, the *function* of fear, in both contexts, must remain constant. In its lower form, fear rests in *malkut*, thus serving as the entrance to the world of the sefirot. At its highest level, fear serves as another kind of entrance—this time, as the gateway to *keter*, the passage out of the sefirot and the world of manifestation. Fear, then, seems intimately connected to the idea of liminality; it is the threshold through which all must pass on their spiritual odysseys. As such, a word such as *awe* (at least in this mystical context) does not exactly capture the force of the phenomenon of *yirah*. It is not so much a sense of awe or reverence that seems to grip the hasidic mystic, as it is the very real *terror of transition* from one state of consciousness to another.

Yaakov Yosef further develops this concept of *yirah* elsewhere in his writings, breaking it up into four discrete subdivisions:

There are [four] different expressions with regard to the matter of fear. Sometimes it is called "the fear of heaven" (*yirat shamayim*), sometimes "the awe of heaven" (*morah shamayim*), sometimes it is called "the fear of God" (*yirat Elohim*), and sometimes "the fear of sin" (*yirat het*). . . . There are two categories of fear—one is internal fear, which comes from love, and [the other] is the fear of the sefirot themselves. Wisdom (*hokhmah*) is called "fear" since one fears to enter the partition of *keter*. Thus the letters of fear (*yirah*) serve as the beginning of the letters of love (*ahavah*) [in that the final letters *alef* and *hey* of *yirah* become the first two letters of the word *ahavah*]: this is to teach us that from fear one enters into love, and from love one enters into internal fear. Thus there are two categories of fear—there is *malkhut*, which is called lower fear, and there is *hokhmah*, which is called internal, or higher, fear. In each one of these [categories] are two [fears], which [create a total of] four types of fear. The first [relates to] that which humans fear from *malkhut*, . . . which is an aspect of the fear of punishment, and is called "the fear of God" (*yirat Elohim*). The other is the fear of *malkhut* itself—the fear of "heaven"—which is *ze'ir anpin*, and is called "the fear of heaven" (*yirat shamayim*). There are also two types of fear [related to] *hokhmah*. The first is the fear of heaven—which comes from *hokhmah*—and is called "high fear" (*yirah ilah*) . . . which means the awe one has for the heaven above. . . . There is also the fear of *hokhmah* itself, which is the fear of the aspect of God, and this fear is called "the fear of sin" (*yirat het*) . . . which comes from the knowledge of one's own deficiency. Understand this.[11]

As far as I am aware, Yaakov Yosef is the first Jewish thinker to delineate the concept of religious fear into such a wide variety of types, each with a different function and value. The approach that he inherited—as seen in the works of figures such as Bakhya ibn Pakudah, Joseph Albo, and Judah Loew—had been to divide religious fear into two basic forms: the fear of punishment (*yirat ha-onesh*) and the fear of God's majesty (*yirat ha-rommemut*). Yaakov Yosef takes this a step further and subdivides these categories into a total of four. The various expressions for religious fear (e.g., the fear of God, the fear of heaven, etc.), which up until Yaakov Yosef seem to have been used almost interchangeably, now take on individual characteristics.

Our author posits two general rubrics from which he describes his four typologies of fear: the "higher" level of fear (which he associates with *hokhmah*), and its "lower" level (associated with *malkhut*). At the highest level of the sefirot, as we have seen, fear springs from love (*binah*) and leads into *keter*. It is this moment of liminality, the consternation one experiences from this passage into the "partition" (*mekhitzah*) of *keter*, that warrants the attachment of the word *fear* to the sefirah of *hokhmah*. In a sense, this dynamic represents the last glimpse of the world of emanation as one crosses into the terra incognita of the Other. It is this kind of fear that Yaakov Yosef calls "internal."

In the "lower" category of fear (which is connected to *malkhut*), love follows from, and does not lead into, fear. Yaakov Yosef joins this fear not to the departure from the world of the sefirot, but to the entrance into it. As such, this category subdivides into distinctions directly related to the divine emanations. The first—and easiest to acquire—type of fear is what Yaakov Yosef calls "the fear of God" (*yirat Elohim*). What one fears here is not the emanation itself (*malkhut*), but an aspect that stems from it. In this case, that aspect is punishment. As we have noted, this is the most primitive and least meritorious of the different kinds of fear. It is connected with *Elohim*, since that divine name is associated with *din*, or judgment/punishment. The second type of lower fear is called "the fear of heaven" (*yirat shamayim*), which is the fear of *malkhut* itself, not of any effect that results from it. The fear of "heaven" is, in fact, the fear of *ze'ir anpin*—the sefirotic world in itself. It is called *yirat shamayim* because it is from the vantage point of *malkhut* that "one will see"[12] (*ye'rayeh*, a pun on *yirah*) *shamayim*, or *ze'ir anpin*.

The first type of "internal" fear is "high fear" (*yirah ilah*, a different phrase for the expression *morah shamayim* mentioned at the outset of the preceding passage), which derives from the awe one has for the heaven above. As in the previous example, this first subdivision relates not to *hokhmah* itself, but to an effect that results from it—in this case, the awe or dread one experiences in the face of the transcendent. The second and highest type of internal fear is "the fear of sin" (*yirat het*).[13] This is the fear of *hokhmah* itself, which is the fear of an aspect of "God Himself" (*elyonah*). That "aspect" is compared to one's own "deficiency," or "lack" (*hisaron*). For Yaakov Yosef, the "fear of sin" carries great existential significance: one becomes aware of one's imperfections, one's finitude, one's "sin" (*het*—that which falls short of its target), when one confronts the perfect, divine Wisdom. The result is fear—the fear of the utter chasm that separates the finite from infinity.

The interplay of the higher- and lower-order fears with the higher- and lower-order loves is complex. Within Yaakov Yosef's spiritual system, there is a clear deference to the kabbalah; he is not, however, reluctant to manipulate the interpretation of the various sefirot if that proves necessary for a sense of coherence in his own schema. Yaakov Yosef was, after all, one of the major disciples of the Baal Shem and a founder of hasidism. His concerns, as Scholem has correctly pointed out,[14] have much more to do with creating a mystical *psychology* than with theosophical speculation. It is not the machinations of the metaphysical world that serve as his focus, but the inner dynamic of the human soul. If the emotion of fear, rather than love, seems more appropriate to describe the shock of transition from one state of consciousness to another, Yaakov Yosef will insert it into his own schematic—even if it necessitates a radical rereading of the kabbalistic tradition itself.

3

Arousal

It is clear that Yaakov Yosef views the responses of
fear and love as partners in an inextricable relationship.
Though at several points that relationship shifts in its
structure and in its power dynamic, the two responses
remain interconnected and interdependent. Yet we have
seen that there are a number of different types of fear
and love, each one a part of either a higher (internal)
or lower (external) order. The previous chapter concen-
trated on the nature of the relation between opposites,
but what of the relationship between those of the *same*
kind? It will be the purpose of the present chapter to
analyze the nature of the spiritual dynamic between the
two orders of religious fear.

There is an inherent tension in the phenomenon
of the encounter between opposites. One is able to
discern this tension in the very structure of the sefirot
(e.g., masculine side versus feminine side, *arikh anpin*
versus *ze'ir anpin*, etc.), and even more so in Yaakov

Yosef's interpretation of them. That tension obviously applies to the notions of fear and love, as we have seen. Quite a different dynamic, however, occurs in the encounter between those of the same kind. In this latter situation, it is an inherent *attraction*, rather than tension, that marks the interaction. This idea of attraction will serve as an important metaphor for understanding Yaakov Yosef's views on the encounter between external and internal fear. In *Ben Porat Yosef*, he writes:

> I heard from my teacher [the Baal Shem], may his memory be a blessing, that a state of fear inheres in all of the worlds and in all of the creatures, and that the root of all of [these fears] is internal fear—the fear of God, may He be blessed. But it is external fear that comes to man in order to arouse him to internal fear. This is God's grace [*ḥesed*], His right hand reaching forth, which asks man to become aroused from [external fear] to the fear of God, as it is written: "What does the Lord thy God ask of thee, but to fear the Lord thy God" (Deu. 10:12)—which is internal fear.[1]

As we noted in chapter two, some condition of fear is part of the entire hierarchy of being. No world or creature is devoid of it. (As we shall see in the next chapter, these simple, or "corporeal," fears are no more than outer garments which mask their true root, which is internal fear, or the fear of God.) Fear of this type is identified with the notion of externality, since even the lowest forms of animal life are able to possess it: no rational faculty is required as its prerequisite. Yet Yaakov Yosef refuses to negate its value. Since it is part of the world of creation, it is ultimately connected, in some way, to God. Though easy to acquire, external fear, as it relates

to human beings, must have some grander teleological
purpose.

The discernment of that purpose is to be found in
the process of *hitorrerut*, or arousal. In the kabbalah,
hitorrerut facilitates the overflow of the divine *shefah*,
or influx, toward man. This influx is associated with
hesed in the right, masculine region of the sefirot. *Shefah*
is the divine vitality, the emission that streams down-
ward as a direct result of human stimulation from the
lower world. But it is also a gift from God, an expression of divine love and benevolence. *Hitorrerut*, the
activity of arousal, describes this dialectic.

How does the idea of fear relate to this whole process? In the kabbalistic context, this *hesed/shefah* is the
source of potential destructiveness. As one writer comments, "finite creatures cannot possibly absorb and en-
dure so abundant and powerful an effulgence as the
divine *hesed*. If exposed to it they would become nulli-
fied in it and cease to exist."[2] This divine influx must
be controlled, restrained, mitigated. *Din*, which is identified with the attribute of fear (and the left, feminine
side of the sefirot), serves this function.

In Yaakov Yosef's system, there seems to be a col-
lapse of this balance. Rather than serving as the counterfoil to the potentially destructive *shefah*, fear (in this case
lower fear, which is joined to *malkhut*) *itself* becomes
the channel through which *hesed* enters the world. External fear is the catalyst that arouses the overflow of the
divine effluence (or, in more psycho-spiritual terminology, God's compassion and grace) into the human arena.
In the kabbalah, as Jacobs makes plain,[3] God gives religious love to man by divine grace only if he strives first
to acquire religious fear. In Yaakov Yosef's view, on

the other hand, fear—even in its lowest form—is impossible to "acquire" through human effort and must therefore be the result of God's undeserved grace. There is no middle step to *hesed*; external fear has become its facilitator.

Yaakov Yosef claims that external fear comes to man in order to "arouse" him to internal fear, i.e., the fear of God. This is an interesting twist in the idea of *hitorrerut* inherited from the kabbalah. We have seen how, at the highest spiritual levels, love precedes and leads into fear. What we see now is that those of the same kind, not only opposites (though in a state of tension), may participate in a relationship. But there is an important difference. With regard to fear and love, this dynamic is possible only if both these responses occur on the same level (e.g., lower fear cannot interact with higher love, and lower love cannot interact with higher fear). Yet, it is possible for lower (external) fear to interact with higher (internal) fear, and to do it in a symbiotic way. This is the result of the resemblance, or "attraction," between them. External fear does not arouse God's *hesed* or even seek to balance it, but instead becomes its very *manifestation*. And it is this manifestation of the divine influx that strives to arouse man to internal fear: the true fear of God.

As we have demonstrated, external fear is ultimately rooted in God, yet has, as its final objective, the fear of that selfsame referent. Yaakov Yosef explores the nature of this unusual process of arousal:

> There is an attribute which is called "the terror of Isaac" (*pakhad Yitzhak*); when this attribute becomes aroused in the upper world, then many kinds of terrors and external fears become aroused in this world. All of this

[occurs] in order to arouse man through [them] to internal fear, [which is] the root of fear [itself].[4]

The attribute of *pakhad Yitzhak* first appears in the
Torah as an expression for God (Gen. 31:42). In the
kabbalistic tradition, Isaac is associated with *gevurah/
din*, the attribute of fear. What this phrase means in
Yaakov Yosef's system is unclear. The "terror of Isaac"
is neither external fear nor the fear of God. It cannot be
external fear, for its first function is to arouse that fear
in this world, and it cannot be the fear of God, since
that is its ultimate goal.

Pakhad Yitzhak seems to serve as a kind of facilitator. It is through its "arousal" in the upper world (presumably via some kind of human effort) that the various types of lower, external fears become aroused in
our world. Then, as the direct result of this process, these
external fears themselves (as manifestations of divine
grace) attempt to arouse man to internal fear which, as
the fear of God, turns out to be the ultimate root of them
all. There is a clear dialectic at work here, a dialectic
which involves both God and man: man arouses the
upper world, the upper world arouses the corporeal
world, and then the corporeal world arouses man to the
fear of God. Yet a question remains: Does man, in the
end, reach the fear of God via his own efforts, or is it
divine grace that is ultimately responsible?

Let us leave this question for a moment and turn
to a passage from the *Toledot*:

It is known that [man] is a microcosm, and through
arousal below the arousal above is brought about. And
the divine influx (*shefah*) will be sent down to the level
of the man who concentrates (*mekhaven*) on it, so that
he receives the divine influx.[5]

The spiritual dialectic here is obvious. The theme of man as a microcosm, a world unto himself, is constant in Yaakov Yosef's writings. It reflects the tendency in the Lurianic kabbalah "to interpret human life and behavior as symbols of a deeper life" and to conceive of man "as a *micro-cosmos* and of the living God as a *macro-anthropos*."[6] In our context, this dialectic of relationship suggests that *hitorrerut* is the encounter between two worlds: man's arousal in his own world leads to the simultaneous arousal of the upper world. There is a direct correlation between human activity below and the overflow of *shefah* (God's gift of grace) from above.

From the phenomenological perspective, this dynamic is somewhat paradoxical. The above passages seem to contend that it is as if man "acquires" the very thing that is *given* to him freely by God. The whole notion of grace is stretched to its breaking point. It remains a gift, an expression of divine benevolence and love which is not deserved, but it is also—and at the same time—the direct result of individual human effort (which is described by Yaakov Yosef as concentration or *kavanah*). It appears that, from these texts, the fear of God is the result of a dialectical process. It is through *hesed*, or divine grace (as manifested by external fears), that man is aroused to this state; yet it is only after he has first aroused the upper world itself that his own arousal can take place. The fear of God is both a gift and an achievement.

We have established that there is a clear relationship between external fear and the fear of God. That connection, however, transcends theosophical structures. In the following text we will see how Yaakov Yosef also establishes a compelling *psychological* linkage:

With regard to the matter of [external] fear, this [occurs] when one fears the absence of glory, wealth, life, and the like. This is not the case after [they are] gone; [then] there is [nothing to] fear, for if one loses [his] life and dies, he can have no fear of the absence of life—and the same applies to wealth when one loses it. This kind of fear is external fear, which can be found in all creatures, for the mouse fears the cat, the cat fears the dog, the dog fears the wolf, and the same with man, who fears his fellow man. Above this [kind of fear] is internal fear, the fear of God, may He be blessed. But it is external fear that comes to man in order to arouse him to internal fear; this is God's grace (*hesed*), His right hand reaching forth, which urges man to become aroused from [external fear] to the fear of God, as it is written, "What does the Lord thy God ask of thee, but to fear the Lord thy God" (Deu. 10:12), which is internal fear. The absence [which relates to] internal fear occurs when one makes himself cleave to God (*hei ha-haim*), and there he [experiences] the Absence of Existence (*heder ha-metzi'ut*). But when one lacks this [kind of] fear, then he will know that he is absent from life (*nedar meha-haim*), [i.e.] that he is already dead.[7]

The critical motif in this passage has to do with the idea of *heder*, or absence. At the lowest levels, one fears the absence, or privation, of some material benefit which one already possesses, such as fame, wealth, or life itself. Even animals are capable of this kind of fear: when a mouse flees from a cat, or a cat from a dog, it is purely out of fear for its own survival. The only difference between human beings and animals in this regard is that humans have more sophisticated objects of desire; we want glory, riches, and love, and not merely life. Yet just as a mouse fears the loss of its

life, so do humans fear the loss of our prized (but material) possessions.

With regard to human beings, this type of fear has
a clear psychological dimension. When one no longer
possesses a particular object of desire (be it fame, wealth,
or love), one can no longer fear its loss. It is gone; there
is no longer any object *over which* to fear. How can one
fear the loss of fame after one has already slid into
obscurity? How can one fear the loss of life after one is
no longer living? External fear is not the fear *of* some
object, but the fear of its absence. It is this *threat* of
privation which serves as the root cause of external fear.
When that threat is removed, whether through the loss
of the object of desire or through the loss of desire for
the object, then the fear itself disappears.

It is this external fear that arouses man to internal
fear. But how does the notion of absence relate to this
latter, and higher, level of fear? The answer is found in
the phenomenon of *devekut*, or adhesion. Yaakov Yosef
uses careful wordplay here in order to put forward an
explanation on two different levels. He claims that a form
of absence occurs when one adheres to God, whom he
calls *hei ha-haim*, or (roughly) "the Lifeblood of Life."
It is through this process of adhesion that one experiences *heder ha-metzi'ut*, the privation of existence. The
result of such a mystical encounter is internal fear, the
response to the threat of the absence of reality.[8] At this
plateau, it is not the potential loss of some material
possession that arouses one's fear, but the very negation of reality itself. In this reading, internal fear shares
a similarity with external fear: both are reactions to the
threat of some type of privation.

Yet there is another reading of this text which allows
for no such similarity. The phrase *heder ha-metzi'ut* is

an expression for God which is perhaps best translated as "the Divine Nought" or "the Holy Nothing" and is associated with *keter*, the highest rung of the sefirotic ladder. To read *heder ha-metzi'ut* as a name, instead of a phenomenon, alters the meaning of the passage in a significant way. Internal fear thus becomes the response to the direct encounter with God Himself, rather than to the threat of reality's privation *as a result* of the event. In this latter case, one still fears the absence of some object; in the former, the fear is *of* an object, namely God, the Absence of Existence. As such, it is the only kind of fear which can accurately be called the fear of God, for it is God Himself whom one fears.[9] To lack this kind of fear is to be absent from "Life," which is to be absent from God. And to be absent from God is to be like one who is already dead.

4

Stripping the Garments

The previous three chapters have been concerned with the clarification of terms and the various aspects of religious fear that relate to functionality. How are lower- and higher-order fears attained? What is the nature of their interdynamic? These questions, and others, help us explore the inner mechanics of the mystic path, the structures and superstructures which the seeker must traverse —and how, in fact, he may traverse them.

Yet these questions of function tell us nothing about the *purpose* of the mystic's strivings. We have gained some insight into what the fear of God is and how the hasid reaches it; now we must address the question of why he makes the effort at all. What is the *goal* of this intricate process of ascent? It is to this last but fundamental question that our fourth and final chapter will turn.

Let us begin, however, with an examination of Yaakov Yosef's treatment of the "garments," the outer veils which the mystic will seek to penetrate and strip away. He writes in the *Toledot* that there are many thousands of levels which relate to the matter of external fear, all of which are [merely] garments for that which is actual: and that root is internal fear, which is the fear of God.[1]

We see here a connection between external, or lower, fear, and the notion of "garments." These garments, the exterior shells that point to and house a far more valuable interior, are almost without number. (One may assume that for every worldly fear there is a parallel garment to mark its presence.) In contradistinction to the nearly limitless quantity of external garments, there is only one true core beneath them, and that is internal fear, the fear of God. This internal fear is the "root" of all other external fears; it is both their foundation and, as we shall see, their ultimate terminus.

Yaakov Yosef writes that

the root of fear is the fear of God, which is [its] inner treasure.[2] Related to this are thousands of levels of external fear, so that man will arrive via [these] garments of fear to internal fear. That is why we call a garment of fear a "house of treasures," for in it is the treasure of the fear of God.[3]

In the previous text we read a descriptive claim that the fear of God is the root beneath the outer garments of external fears. Here we have a prescriptive claim, that a man must use these garments as *paths* to inner fear. The fear of God is a hidden treasure; to reach it we must first penetrate its protective walls. Yaakov Yosef makes this point clearly:

All of the types of fear that exist in the world do so in order to give man the knowledge to understand that they were created as garments so that [he would] arrive at their inner root, and fear God, may He be blessed.[4]

The implication of this passage seems to be that outer, worldly fears exist for a single purpose: to help bring man to their true root, the fear of God. They are not ends in themselves, but means to an end. In themselves, they have no particular importance; they gain their value only with regard to their special and primary *function*, which is as vehicles for spiritual ascent. Once the potential mystic comes to grasp this, he may begin his journey.

In order to appreciate more fully the final purpose of religious fear, it is necessary to examine a bit further the concept of the fear of God as the root from which other fears stem. Our author writes:

Man is himself a microcosm, and when the Mishnah states "Know that which is higher than you" (Avot 2:1), it means to say that, from a matter that is below, one may discern that which is above. For sometimes there falls upon a man some fear of authority, or of wicked men, or of robbers; at those times he should make his soul cleave with the root of fear, which is the fear of God, may He be blessed. . . . This fear falls upon him in order to arouse him, since he should fear his sins, for "the sinners of Zion are afraid" (Is. 33:14), and make his heart return, and fear with the fear of God, may He be blessed. Then he connects all the levels of fear through himself until [they reach] their root above.[5]

We find at the outset of this passage the covert confirmation of the claim that was made at the close of chapter two: Yaakov Yosef, like other hasidim, was more interested in creating a mystical psychology than with theosophy as such. The phrase that "man is himself a microcosm" (*adam hu olam katan*) is one that surfaces over and over again in our author's writings. In its various contexts, and through the way in which the sefirot are used as psycho-spiritual, as opposed to metaphysical, attributes, there seems to be a human *interiorization* of the sefirot taking place in Yaakov Yosef's religious schema. The clear implication is that man therefore becomes a "universe" unto himself.

Yaakov Yosef interprets the mishnaic statement to "know that which is higher than you" to mean that one may come to understand the supernal realms from that which transpires in the lower, corporeal world. For the kabbalists, human activity in the physical world manipulates divine activity in the metaphysical world. Here, Yaakov Yosef makes the further claim that actual discernment of the higher realms is possible via their *traces* in the world of the mundane. He elaborates on this notion in his discussion of fear.

When a man experiences one of the myriad lower forms of fear, e.g., the fear of power, the fear of harm, etc., he has one of two alternatives. He may do nothing, and treat those fears as complete/actualized in themselves. He may, on the other hand (and, according to Yaakov Yosef, should), seek to transcend them or, more correctly, have the vision to see beyond them. In our author's system, those lower fears are but the outer, illusory garments of their true root, the fear of God to which the hasid should cleave. The fear of the mundane thus serves, in its essence, as a trace of the fear (and also the reality) of the supramundane, and it is this subtle knowledge that the true hasid will come to fathom. Where the masses see only shadow, the mystic seeks the light that lies behind its generation.

As we mentioned in the preceding chapter, the phenomenon of *arousal* punctuates the relation between the lower and higher forms of fear. When one of the lower, external fears falls upon the hasid, he should strive to adhere to its actual root, to make his heart return to the source that underlies his trepidation. If this spiritual excavation is successful, then he becomes aware of the fact that what he essentially fears is not object *x* or *y*, but none other than God Himself. All of this activity takes place within the "small world" of the individual soul. If it is successful, this inner process results in the interconnection of all external fears with their root above.

What is the consequence for the hasid of this dynamic of interconnection? Yaakov Yosef continues:

> [After the interconnection,] then there is no [more] dread, and fears will no longer fall upon him, for they have become sweetened by their root. This is what is meant by "What does the Lord require of thee, but to fear the Lord thy God?" [Deu. 10:12]. After you have connected all of the many types of fears in the world with the singular fear of God, they will then become negated from you.[6]

Here we have our first, and rather radical, statement on the effect of this entire process on the life of the individual hasid. The connection of external fears with the fear of God—their true root—leads directly, and necessarily, to the *negation* of those fears. The excavative approach strives to unite the lower, immediate forms of fear (e.g., the fear of authority, the fear of loss, etc.) with their higher, generative (but mediated) foundation. It is not possible to reach the root fear of God without first digging through its outer manifestations or traces. Though these garments can often be bitter, the process of interconnection *sweetens* them as they unite with their root. The pain of worldly fears is negated as one sees beyond them; this leads to the cessation of even the fear of them.

This seems to be, *prima facie*, one of the fundamental goals of the hasidic God-fearer: the transcendence of the fears of the world. With each garment he strips away, the closer he comes to its realization. Yet, as we have seen, for Yaakov Yosef, the phenomenon of fear is only complete and fully effective in its relation to the phenomenon of love. Love must play a role in negation as in other psychic processes. With this in mind, he expands on how this dynamic operates, using more theosophical/kabbalistic terminology. In a comment on the biblical commandment "Thou shalt love the Lord thy God" (Deu. 6:5)—which parallels and precedes the commandment to fear God—Yaakov Yosef writes, in the name of the Baal Shem Tov:

> What can it matter to God whether or not we love Him? Of what value is it to a great king if a tiny, insignificant insect loves him? Now the world was created through *din*, which is the secret of the divine withdrawal (*tzimtzum*), as is known. Therefore, man's judgments (*diney ha-adam*) and torments [the worldly fears] are the body for the soul and the spiritual vitality. When a man accepts these torments with love and joy—since they are an aspect of the spiritual vitality—he makes the body conjoin with and adhere to the soul, which is the spiritual vitality. [In this way] the judgment is negated.[7]

Why should God care whether or not human beings love (or, for that matter, fear) Him? Why would the Torah issue such commandments? In his answer to these questions, we see how Yaakov Yosef uses the notion of love as an integral element in the process of the negation of fears. The world was created through the attribute of *din*, which is the "secret" that lies behind the concept of God's withdrawal from the world. God had no choice but to absent Himself from the world of man; the finite world would not have been able to bear the full splendor of the infinite. This judgment, rooted in God's love for His creatures, is the source of all judgments. The pains and sufferings of the world (which man fears and dreads) are the price he must pay for existence. They are the outer shell, the body of the soul—the products of God's love for him, and the only way he is able to survive.

The implication of this conception of pain and suffering is an almost Augustinian position on the problem of the world's evils. According to this view, evil has no true reality in itself but is merely the privation, or *absence*, of good. (Needless to say, this move is extremely problematic and, in a post-Holocaust world, seemingly untenable.) This worldview leads Yaakov Yosef—who himself was no stranger to suffering—to the conclusion that it is through the acceptance or, better, the embrace of such pain that causes its ultimate negation. By loving God, which is here equated with accepting His judgments (as the quasi-"manifestations" of God's withdrawal)[8], the body adheres to the soul and the spiritual vitality/divine grace begins to flow. It is this flow which drowns the agony of the myriad types of external fear.

Yaakov Yosef uses the notion of negation not only with reference to nullifying lower forms of fear. He writes that

the righteous possess both internal love and internal fear. This is why the Torah states, "Thou shalt love the

Lord thy God" [Deu. 6:5], since one must love His torments and sufferings. It also [states]: "Fear the Lord thy
God" [Deu. 10:20], which is the result of the attribute
of *din*. If this is the case [that the righteous possess both
qualities of love and fear], it [derives] from God's glory
and greatness, may He be blessed, for there is no pause
to this kind of love and fear—even if they are wounded
by the attribute of *din*. Yet what is the path to love and
to fear God? Through the way we mentioned previously,
namely, "When one reflects on God's deeds and creatures . . . one is immediately [filled with] love [for God]
. . . And when one contemplates these things, one immediately trembles and grows fearful. . . ."[9] This means
to say that when [one possesses both] love and fear
together, the difference [between them] is negated.[10]

This passage serves as the climax to Yaakov Yosef's
discussion in the *Toledot* of the relationship between
the love and fear of God. He claims that the righteous
possess both of them. Love is their response to the
external fears, and fear is the result of the attribute of
din (which is the secret behind *tzimtzum*, the expression of God's love for man). Both of these responses
derive from the reality of God, though each relates to a
different aspect of His personality: love stems from the
experience of God's "glory," while fear corresponds to
the experience of His "greatness." Since these aspects
of God are without limit, so too is the intensity and
the constancy of the responses to them—even if, for
instance, one is "wounded" by one of the judgments or
torments that are a necessary feature of the human
world.

How does one achieve these internal affects? Yaakov Yosef returns to Maimonides to find the answer,
yet seems to reread him in a profound way. It is through

metaphysical contemplation that one comes to love and fear God, argues the Rambam, and since love relates to epistemic awareness, while fear is rooted in the more primitive existential consciousness, there is a very serious distinction between the two, as well as an order of supremacy. Yaakov Yosef obliterates such distinctions. While earlier he supports the Maimonidean position in its plain sense,[11] we see in the above text a different interpretation of it. At the highest spiritual levels, the distinctions between fear and love dissolve, and the two coalesce into a single totality. Neither is superior to the other; the very *notion* of otherness is negated, as the fear of God and the love of God merge and become indistinguishable.

We noted before that negation only seems, *prima facie*, to be a key goal of the mystic's quest. In fact, it is not a goal at all. That the mystic is able to transcend his fears of the world through the fear of God is clear; yet this is merely an incidental benefit of the primary, and actual, goal, which is internal fear. The fear of God is not the means to an end—negation—but rather an end in itself:

> When a man understands that [external fears] are [the expressions of] God's grace and love, may He be blessed, who sends external fear in order to arouse him to internal fear, then his fear transforms into love, for he accepts with love the external fear. At that time, external fear is negated; if, however, the man's intent in the matter was [only] to negate external fear, then he has achieved nothing. This is what the Torah warns against: "Thou shalt love the Lord thy God with all thy heart" [Deu. 6:5], [which means that a man] must have a whole heart when external fear comes [to him]; "with all thy soul, and with all thy might"

[Deu. 6:5], [which means that he] must possess the appropriate intent. Understand this.[12]

The consciousness of the reality that worldly fears are but the manifestations of God's grace—and the necessary result of His withdrawal—leads directly to the metamorphosis of fear into love. This dynamic relates to the lower levels of these affects, for, as we have seen, at their respective peaks there is an ultimate coalescence of the two. When one is able to *love* his fears (which is only possible with the knowledge of the "secret" of *tzimtzum*), then there is a negation of those selfsame fears.

There is a critical restriction, however, to this entire process: the negation of external fears cannot be the impetus for the mystic's efforts. Yaakov Yosef introduces the notion of *intentionality* to the phenomenon of negation. To fear God for the sake of an extrinsic benefit is itself a fear of inferior worth; it is analogous to the slave who serves his master not out of love, but in the expectation of some reward. True fear of God is not the avoidance of suffering but the embrace of divinity. The negation of fear/pain is strictly a secondary outcome of this sentiment.

Yet what if the potential mystic *does* intend to fear God only for the sake of its extrinsic benefit? Will the phenomenon of negation still occur? On this point Yaakov Yosef is unclear. In the case of such an event, our author writes: *lo ma-haney klum.* This phrase seems to have two possible translations: either it means (roughly) "it is of no merit," or it means "nothing derives from it." I do not know if Yaakov Yosef intended to be ambiguous about this problem, but the Hebrew certainly is. Either he is saying that the mystic, though a beneficiary of negation, has in fact accomplished nothing of real spiritual worth, or he is claiming that the very event of negation will not occur in such a situation. The answer is ambiguous. What is clear is that intentionality relates to *moral* merit. Whether or not the lack of such merit will prevent the occurrence of a mystical operation remains an open question (and is, in fact, part of the wider problem of the relationship between ethics and mysticism in general).

If the negation of human pain is not the goal of the true hasidic mystic, then what is? In order to understand this final purpose, we must look to the story of the Exodus from Egypt. The Torah makes it clear that the real purpose of Israel's liberation from bondage is not simply to escape Pharaoh, but rather to serve God.[13] That Israel is freed from their enslavement in Egypt is, of course, significant, yet that freedom gains its significance only in relation to the fact that its function is to bring Israel into the wilderness for divine service. If Moses is the paradigm for Yaakov Yosef's notion of the zaddik and mediation, then the Exodus episode as a whole serves as his metaphor for the mystical experience. Writes our author:

> "And it came to pass in the course of those many days" [Ex. 2:23]; this means that [Israel experienced] many days of despair and torments because of evil, external fear, and [only] afterwards became aroused to internal fear. "And the king of Egypt died" [Ex. 2:23], which is the death of their distress and the negation of their exile in Egypt.[14]

Here we see the equation of Pharaoh and exile (*galut*) with external fear. The Exodus from Egypt is implicitly compared to the arousal to internal fear, which leads directly to the death/negation of Pharaoh, of distress, and of exile. The passage continues:

> "And the children of Israel sighed because of the bond-age (*min ha-avodah*)" [Ex. 2:23]; this describes Israel in relation to *avodah*, which [means] divine service. "And the children of Israel cried out" [Ex. 2:23], for they were not able to worship God or to adhere to the fear and service of Him, may He be blessed. Then "their cry rose up to God because of the bondage (*min ha-avodah*)" [Ex. 2:23]; all of this was due to the mediation of Moses, which is why immediately following [these verses] it is written, "Now Moses was the shepherd of Jethro's flock" [Ex. 3:1]. Deliverance came through him. . . . Understand that Moses took Joseph's quality (*midat Yosef*) [with him], and, as a result, deliverance came to Israel through his hand. . . .[15]

In a remarkable interpretation of the word *avodah*, Yaakov Yosef makes the claim that it is not the pain of enslavement itself, but the inability to serve God, which is the source of Israel's despair. What Israel yearns for is union with its God, rather than relief from its toil. The bones that Moses/the zaddik carries with him are Joseph's essential nature: the embodiment of the fear of God and the vehicle that will bring Israel to its final goal. Thus, though the negation of suffering is impor-tant, the real purpose of the Exodus episode—and, by extension, of the mystic quest itself—is Israel's deliver-ance, not from Egypt, but into the hands of God. The fear of God will provide the path to its actualization.

Yaakov Yosef spiritualizes the story of the Exodus. No longer solely an historical event, it becomes, for him, a paradigm for personal, mystical redemption that tran-scends time and place:

Just as it was in the Egyptian exile, so it is in this bitter
exile. Just as there was redemption in Egypt, . . . so there
will be [redemption] in every man and in every age.
And "as in the days of thy coming out of the land of
Egypt, I will show them marvellous things" [Micah 7:15].
Amen. Selah.[16]

II

THE GREAT MAGGID: DOV BAER OF MEZERITCH

The extremist tendencies that are found in the Maggid's phenomenology predate his embrace of hasidism. As a young man, Dov Baer (d. 1772) practiced an ascetic regimen of such severity that he often fell ill from it. Legend has it that, after one particularly grave illness, the Maggid made a pilgrimage to Miedzyboz to seek out the Baal Shem Tov, whose renown as a healer was widespread. It was after this encounter, so the legend goes, that the Maggid abandoned his asceticism and became a key figure in the Baal Shem Tov's inner circle.

As we have noted, it was the Maggid, and not the more senior Yaakov Yosef, who became the successor of the Baal Shem Tov after his death in 1760. Unlike his master, who was able to popularize hasidic teachings, the Maggid's talent lay in his ability to influence scholars, whether kabbalists or rabbis. Despite the radicality and elitism of the Maggid's speculative mysticism, he gathered around himself an army of disciples, "young men whose zeal had not been cooled by scholastic pursuits, and old men who had not found inner solace in either revealed or hidden wisdom."[1] Their names are impressive: Levi Yitzhak of Berdichev, Shneur Zalman of Lyady, Nahum of Chernobyl, Elimelekh of Lyzhansk, and others.

As opposed to Yaakov Yosef, the Maggid rarely cites the words of the Baal Shem Tov. His writings, though rooted in kabbalistic terminology, are highly original and innovative. As a mystic, the Maggid is less interested in issues of ethics and piety than with purely spiritual, and often even quietistic, contemplative activity. As a phenomenologist, the Maggid is concerned with understanding three primary aspects of *unio mystica*: how one attains the mystical event, the nature of the event itself, and the effects of the event on the mystic. As we shall see, the fear of God plays a critical role in the entire process.

To discover the Maggid's views on this subject, we must follow the same methodological procedure that was used for our study of Yaakov Yosef, namely, an analysis of his homiletical and theoretical writings. The most important collection is found in *Maggid Devarav le-Yaakov*, or *Likutei Amarim* (Lvov, 1792); his other works include *Or ha-Emet* and *Shemuah Tovah* (both compiled by Levi Yitzhak of Berdichev), *Or Torah*, and *Likutei Yekarim*. The dating of these books is problematic, primarily because they were not written down by the Maggid himself, but by his various disciples in a variety of versions.

Our examination of the Maggid's views on religious fear is divided into four chapters. Chapter one explores his use (and transformation) of the kabbalistic notion of *tzimtzum*, or "contraction." Chapter two concentrates on some of the Maggid's lengthier sermons on fear and its acquisition, as well as on the role of analogy in his system. Chapter three analyzes the notion of *ayin* (nothingness) and its relationship to the mystical event, and chapter four focuses on the effects and aftereffects of that event on the person of the mystic.

1

Tzimtzum: Contraction as Relationship

It is clear that the phenomenon of mediation is of critical import to Yaakov Yosef's spiritual system. Not only does it allow for the masses to reach the point of adhesion with God, but it serves as the unitive force which makes possible the interrelationship of opposites. Yet is this notion relevant to the Maggid's thought, where the doctrine of the zaddik is not emphasized? Though the Maggid recognizes that mystical encounter may occur without the help of a mediator, we shall see that mediation itself *does*, in fact, still play a role in his phenomenology.

The Maggid discusses an aspect of this issue in a passage on the Torah's entrance into the world. He writes in the *Maggid Devarav le-Yaakov*:

> It is known that the Torah is called a "flying scroll" [BT Gittin 60a]. This is because it is greater than all the worlds [of emanation]; God [therefore], may He be blessed, needed to contract (*le-tzamtzem*) the Torah so that He would be able to make the light of the

Torah shine in the worlds. . . . God, may He be blessed, needed to contract the Torah through the attribute of fear, which is called "contraction" (*tzimtzum*). This is analogous to a man who "fears" (*yarey*) his friend, and is "shamed" (*bosh*) before him; [thus] he shrinks (*maktin*) and contracts (*metzamtzem*) himself.[1]

At this point, the Maggid posits a description of the world's encounter with the Torah, not of *unio mystica* per se. The Torah enters the world through its own contraction; as a divine "text" which transcends the worlds of emanation, it must of necessity be contracted (by God) so that it can penetrate, and not overwhelm, those very worlds. This scenario intimates the Lurianic ideas of *tzimtzum* and *shevirah*, the "breaking of the vessels," through which the divine "sparks" enter the world. In this context, God contracts the Torah—and not Himself—so that the world may bear its light.

The attribute by which God effects this contraction is that of fear, which itself is called *tzimtzum*. The Maggid presents an analogy to better understand this unusual association: when a man "fears," and is "shamed" before, his friend, he makes himself recoil, or shrink, from that friend's presence. In a similar way, the Torah is made to shrink from the world in order to enter into it. It must be pointed out that the words *fear* and *shame* make no sense with regard to *tzimtzum*, if taken at their face value; they are, instead, technical terms for extremely sophisticated responses to the phenomenon of encounter. We will discuss this topic in relation to the following passage:

Interconnection (*hitkashrut*) comes as a result of [shrinkage], that is to say wisdom, for one cannot connect himself to his friend unless he shrinks himself and consid-

ers himself as nothing (*ayin*) compared to him. . . . And
the cause of this quality of interconnection is the quality of fear.[2]

In this text we find a clear expression of one of the
Maggid's most unique teachings: that of the paradoxical
connection through contraction. As Scholem comments,
in the Lurianic school, *tzimtzum* "does not mean the
concentration of God *at* a point, but His retreat *away*
from a point. . . . God was compelled to make room for
the world by, as it were, abandoning a region within
himself."[3] The Maggid transforms this divine notion of
contraction into the metaphor for *all* interpersonal encounters. Just as the first act of God—the Infinite Being—
is a movement of recoil, or withdrawal into Himself, so
(for the Maggid) is this contraction fundamental to any
meeting between beings.

Inherent in every ontological encounter is the collision of being, or what I will refer to as the "ontic
assault." This phenomenon, though necessarily violent,
is also the prerequisite for intimacy. (As we shall see, at
the level of divine-human confrontation, or *unio mystica*, such violence reaches its most profound expression.) It is only by taking a step back, through the
"shrinkage" of one's very self, that true relationship
becomes possible. One must "make room" for the other;
interconnection can only result from self-contraction,
from the mediation of being itself.

The ability to contract, or shrink oneself, reaches
full fruition when one thinks of oneself as "nothing," or
ayin (a technical idea we shall explore in chapter three).
There is a striking causality between self-conception and
self-contraction: to view oneself as "nothing" actually
creates the emptiness out of which nondestructive inti-

macy may emerge (after the initial shock of the ontic assault). The Maggid gives the doctrine of *creatio ex nihilo* a strange twist: whereas "the creation of heaven and earth brought being (*yesh*) from nothingness (*ayin*), the zaddikim make nothingness from being."[4] The process as a whole is linked to wisdom, which in turn is linked to fear. Just as Yaakov Yosef joined fear to the sefirah of *hokhmah*, so does the Maggid. In the latter's system, however, this sefirah receives two additional, and more phenomenological, identifications—*ayin* and *tzimtzum*.

Yet how, precisely, does fear relate to the notion of contraction and thus to the phenomenon of encounter? The Maggid explains:

> If there had been no contraction (*tzimtzum*), human beings would not have been able to receive God's brightness (*behiruto*), or withstand His greatness, and would have been annihilated from existence. It is known (*Etz Haim*, gate 18, chapter 5) that the attribute of fear is that which contracts and [imposes] limits, and all this occurs through wisdom, within which [fear] is clothed. It is written, "The beginning of wisdom is the fear of the Lord" (Ps. 111:10), for it is known (Zohar, Lev. 17a) that wisdom is [the letter] *yod*, the smallest of all the letters, since it shrinks and contracts itself because it is the first of them all, and close to the Cause of all Causes [here associated with the sefirah of *keter*]. . . . Because it is close to God (*Eyn Sof*), out of great fear and shame it contracts and restricts itself; this shame causes fear and *tzimtzum*, for fear comes as a result of its own sense of lowliness (*shifluto*), as well as from the necessity to contract so that the lower creatures will be able to receive it.[5]

Without divine contraction, humanity would have been obliterated, unable to withstand God's *behirut*, or "brightness." It is the attribute of fear which confers the ability to contract, restrict, and limit; it is fear, therefore, which underlies the act of *tzimtzum*. At this point, the Maggid has not departed from the kabbalah, which views the sefirah of *din*/judgment (connected to fear) as integral to the process of God's contraction from the world. As Scholem writes, "inasmuch as *tzimtzum* signifies an act of negation and limitation it is also an act of judgment."[6] For the Maggid, however, the marriage of this particular *kind* of fear to the phenomenon of *tzimtzum* is unacceptable.

Fear itself is couched in the garment of wisdom, an attribute not placed within the trunk of the sefirotic tree but at its very apex (as we will see, the Maggid makes little distinction between the sefirot of *hokhmah* and *keter*). The act of contraction thus takes place at the most profound, elevated levels of divinity. Being so close to God, or Eyn Sof, the sefirah of wisdom experiences "shame" in its presence, a response that will lead directly to fear and ultimate contraction. This *tzimtzum*, which allows for the emergence of the rest of the sefirot, occurs for two reasons: first, from the self-consciousness of the sefirah's own lowliness (compared to Eyn Sof) and, second, as the necessary condition for the world's existence.

The Maggid writes elsewhere:

"The eye of the Lord is upon those who fear Him" [Ps. 33:18]: this is written in the singular. "The eyes of the Lord are upon the zaddikim" [Ps. 34:16]: this is written in the plural. It is also written, "Wisdom (*hakhmot*) cries aloud in the street" (Prov. 1:20); there are two [types of wisdom], high wisdom (*hokhmah ilah*) and low wisdom (*hokhmah tatah*), and there are [two corresponding types of fear,] internal fear (*yirah penimiyut*) and external fear (*yirah hitzoniyut*). External [fear] is the fear that falls upon one when he beholds [God's] greatness. . . . Internal fear [occurs] when one recognizes His inner essence and significance, and also that one is as nothing (*ayin*) in importance compared to Him. . . . Thus one is shamed before Him, as it is written about Moses, may peace be upon him, "and they were afraid to come near him" (Ex. 34:30); this means that they knew him from before, but now saw the radiance that was upon him. [Then] they recognized his superiority over them [both] in [spiritual] level and in importance, and were therefore shamed in his presence. This is called the fear of shame (*yirah bushah*). . . . These two fears correspond to high wisdom and low wisdom, which is *malkhut*. . . . In order to attain the fear of shame one must recognize and understand [God's] divinity (*elohut*), may He be blessed. This is impossible without *tzimtzum*, for [God] contracts Himself, as it were, so that one will be able to grasp Him; yet this contraction is also impossible unless the man shrinks himself, for, like water, one "face" enters the other. . . . Divine contraction is impossible without love, and thus the fear of shame is more internal than love, and above it at [the level of] high wisdom. . . . And this is the meaning of "The eyes of the Lord are upon the zaddikim": there are two [types of] wisdom, high wisdom, and low wisdom, which relate to [two types of] fear, and the zaddik possesses both of them. The verse "the eye of the Lord is upon those who fear Him," however, refers to the man who [merely] fears; [there is mention in it of] only one [eye], and this is external fear.[7]

In an interpretation of two verses from Psalms, the Maggid claims that there exist two specific kinds of wisdom, *hokhmah ilah* and *hokhmah tatah*. As we noted previously, each contains an associated fear. The lower, external fear is the result of the brush with God's greatness (presumably His sheer existence), while the higher,

internal fear is the response to insight into His true essence
and one's sense of personal insignificance left in its wake.
External fear corresponds to the sefirah of *malkhut*, while
internal fear is rooted in that of *hokhmah* itself. Though
the man of simple faith may possess the former attribute,
only in the zaddik do the two inhere together.

The Maggid here makes a radical departure from
the kabbalah, and from Yaakov Yosef, as well. We have
shown how Yaakov Yosef connects God's "manifestations of absence" (or, for him, external fears) with *hesed*
and *malkhut*, and in this chapter we have discussed how
the kabbalists associate the divine contraction with *din*,
or *gevurah*. On this issue, the Maggid takes a completely
novel approach: the act of God's withdrawal occurs not
in the lowest or middle regions of the sefirot, but at their
peak. It ceases to be merely an automatic, ontological
chain reaction and instead becomes a deliberate act of
God's own will.

In order to reach the highest level of fear, which
the Maggid calls the "fear of shame," one must come to
fathom God's essential nature, or divinity (*elohut*). This
is beyond intellectual apprehension and can only occur
through a twofold process of *tzimtzum*. God must first
contract Himself. From the divine perspective, this act
of *tzimtzum* is a concealment, but from the human point
of view, it is a *revelation*. And it is revelatory knowledge alone that can offer insight into the divine personality. To receive this revelation, however, a second
tzimtzum must occur: the receiver himself must "shrink"
before God. When one becomes "as nothing," when one
experiences the fear of shame, then, like the merger of
two bodies of water, one is able to merge with God.[8]

Though the fear of shame, or *yirah ilah*, is on a
higher spiritual level than love, this latter attribute is its

prerequisite, and without it, contraction (and therefore *unio mystica*) could not take place. The Maggid conveys this point through the use of analogies, which he views as fundamental for spiritual knowledge: "The parable is the vessel for understanding."[9] Let us examine one such parable below:

> A parable about a rabbi who teaches his student: if the student trembles at the words of his rabbi, and inclines his heart towards these words, [then] the rabbi is able to reveal, and open for him, the doors to the gates of wisdom, even though he will not be able to teach him all of his great and mighty wisdom. . . . Thus [the rabbi] needs to shrink his wisdom so that it will be [rendered] comprehensible to the student.[10]

The only way that a pupil will be able to begin to grasp the teachings of his rabbi is through a twofold process. First, he must love and fear his mentor, and thus become receptive to his message; second, there must be an act of *tzimtzum*, in this case, the contraction of the rabbi's wisdom. What the rabbi shows him is merely the threshold, the "doors to the gates" of his knowledge; he must first "filter," or *mediate*, the intensity of his wisdom if any real intellectual contact is to occur between them. The motivation for this act of contraction is love, like the love of a father for his son:

> It is written, "and you shall make two cherubim (*keruvim*)" [Ex. 25:18]; as our sages said, *keravya* [a play on the word *ke-ravya*, "like an infant"]. That is, such is the way of the father who, because of his love for the child, distorts his speech and speaks in the manner of a child, or contracts his intellect into that of the child. We therefore find that the father is on the level of [the

intellect of] the son, and that explains "and you shall make two cherubim."[11]

Just as love is the prerequisite for the fear of shame (on the human level), so is love the foundation for the fear/contraction that occurs in God. In essence, these two responses are indispensable to the transcendence of the ontic assault, or fundamental violence of the interpersonal encounter. Schatz-Uffenheimer writes that "it is difficult [I would argue dangerous] for man to comprehend 'God'—i.e., the Divinity in its full, un-contracted sense—but the Godhead as contracted . . . may be encountered through means of mediation."[12] The rabbi contracts his teachings, and the father his words, out of a *fear* for the well-being of the student/son: each "comes down" to the level of his receiver to protect and not overwhelm him. The impetus mingles both fear and love. *Tzimtzum* (at the divine level) results from the fear not *of* an object, but out of the fear *for* an object. From the human standpoint, however, one's fearful recoil from God's essence—the fear of shame—is precisely the act which creates the space in which to receive His revelation, though it, too, springs from love.

Unlike the kabbalists, the Maggid associates the divine contraction with the sefirah of *hokhmah*, as opposed to *hesed* and *gevurah*. Moreover, we have shown that the attribute of internal fear—*yirah ilah*—is inextricably linked to, or, better, identical with, this uppermost sefirotic region of wisdom. Yet the Maggid still connects the notion of fear to the above middle sefirot, albeit a fear of an inferior kind:

There is a [type of spiritual] fear analogous to [what we mean] when we say, "so and so is afraid to leave his father," . . . for this is *gevurah* within *hesed*, [or] fear

that is within love. [In this case] one fears to be sepa-
rated from [God], may He be blessed, out of great love
[for Him]. Yet there is a problem: if the fear of separation from [God], may He be blessed, exists, then this
proves that there is the possibility of separation from
Him. Why would the Creator, blessed be He, create the
potential for separation from Him? This is the answer:
if a son is always with his father, then there is no pleasure [in it] for the father. This is the general rule: a
constant pleasure is no pleasure. By way of analogy, if
a man eats fowl every day, it ceases [to be] pleasur-
able. Therefore, if a man [first] distances himself from
his father, and afterwards draws near [to him], then
[his father] will have great pleasure. The parallel is
obvious.[13]

In yet another father/son parable, the Maggid contends that though the son's fear of leaving his father's
side is motivated by his love for him, it is an immature
fear, and of little ultimate merit. The Maggid joins this
inferior response to *gevurah* and *hesed*—a kind of fear
"within" love. For the kabbalists, this is the level of the
great *tzimtzum*; for the Maggid, it represents the fear
of a child. The spiritually mature mystic will know that
it is only through self-contraction (or "distance" in the
preceding text) that a true, and healthy, relationship with
God is possible. In order to receive God's revelation,
the mystic must make room for it.

Is it possible, however, for the mystic to actually
compel such a revelation? The Maggid thinks the answer
is yes:

With [a man's] thought and intent, he makes a throne
for the Holy One, blessed be He; when he thinks with
the love [of God], may He be blessed, he makes [God]

dwell in the World of Love, and when he thinks with
the fear of God, may His name be blessed, he makes
Him dwell in the World of Fear. A man must not stop
thinking of God, may He be blessed, for even a single
moment; through this [process] he makes the Holy One,
blessed be He, dwell within him.[14]

When a man contemplates God, he prepares a "throne"
for Him, or a space in which He may be present. There
is a direct correlation between the *type* of thought that
a man thinks and the "world" into which God enters. If
one's thought is related to love, then God is made to
dwell in the World of Love; if it relates to fear, then God
resides in the World of Fear. As we will see, if the mystic is able to think of "nothing," or *ayin* (which represents the annihilation of discursive thought altogether),
then God is made to dwell within the mystic himself.
As Schatz-Uffenheimer writes,

> The Godhead does not "think" as a separate persona
> with its own thoughts, but it manifests itself as the
> source of thought. More than it thinks itself, it is thought
> by man or "contracted" within his intellect. . . . In
> the final analysis, *tzimtzum* is the way by which the
> human intellect forces God, by His own laws of exist-
> ence, to appear within it."[15]

With a new interpretation of a verse cited previously, the Maggid himself writes:

> And this is the interpretation of "The eyes of the Lord
> are upon the zaddikim" [Ps. 34:16]. Just as the son, when
> he performs an act of youthful [foolishness], brings the
> intellect of his father within those deeds, so do they
> cause the Holy One, blessed be He, [to enter,] as it were,

into the image of their intellects, so that He must think what they think. If they think with love, they bring the Holy One, blessed be He, into the World of Love, as the Zohar comments [on the verse] "The King is trapped in the tresses" [Songs 7:6]—[this means] "the tresses of the mind."[16] The Holy One, blessed be He, dwells where [the human being] thinks and the intellect is called "the eye [of God]," and it is in the hands of the zaddikim. But how does one merit this level? By thinking that he is dust, and unable to act at all without the power of the Holy One, blessed be He. Yet we find that what he does is, [in fact,] done by the Holy One, blessed be He, for were it not for Him, may He be blessed, he would be unable to do anything.[17]

Does this passage refute the possibility of autonomous thought? Schatz-Uffenheimer writes that "the more man is able to experience the dialectical concept of dominance over and submission to the divine element within himself, the more the horizon of his spiritual ability expands"[18]—i.e., to think the Godhead in its contracted manifestation, while "freeing" it from the prison of its limitation. The mystic who has contracted God within his own thought liberates Him from the "tresses of the mind" at the point of *unio mystica*. The text betrays a clear elitism: the intellect (or the "eye" of God) is the possession of the zaddik/mystic alone, and only he has the ability to prepare the space in which God may become manifest.

We are left with a paradox. When a man contracts his mind (e.g., thinks that he is "dust"), he forces the contraction/revelation of God; yet that very contraction, the Maggid argues, is actually the work of God Himself. How do we make sense of this problem? The Maggid writes:

"Your God is a high priest" [BT Sanhedrin 39a]: this means that [God] serves Himself. For due to the power of thought that is given [to man] from the World of Thought, and [the power] of speech [that is given to him] from the World of Speech, man [is able to] think and speak.[19]

God ultimately serves Himself through the vessel of man. When a man thinks, or when he speaks, it is only as the result of the divine immanent reality acting within him. In the words of Friedrich Schleiermacher, man is in an existential state of "absolute dependence" upon his Creator. The moment of mystical union, therefore, is not truly a "possession" of the mystic by God, but more a "release" of the divine potentiality that is already a part of him. It is the mystic, and he alone, who understands—and therefore sets into motion—this irruption of infinity.

2

Interpretations
and Analogies

We observed in part one that Yaakov Yosef grounds
his typological analysis in two fundamental categories
of fear: *yirat ha-onesh* (the fear of punishment) and *yirat
ha-rommemut* (the fear of God's majesty). Though his
homilies on the subject are informative from a theological perspective, they offer us little insight into the phe-
nomenal *outcomes* of the different responses. In general, the Maggid adheres to the same classical distinctions
between lower- and higher-order fears; where he departs
from them, however, is in his focus on the effects of
these responses on the existential relationship between
God and man. He writes:

> "The counsel of the Lord is with them that fear Him,
> and He will reveal to them His covenant" [Ps. 25:14]. It
> is known that the treasure of a king is not silver or
> gold—for they matter little to him—but rather that than
> which nothing is more important. What, then, is the
> "treasure" of a king? It is fear, that all the nations will
> fear him. This is his pleasure, and he has no pleasure

greater than this. Thus, "the fear of the Lord is His treasure" [Is. 33:6] means that fear is the foundation of the
treasure—the fear of God, which is *yirat ha-rommemut*,
and not *yirat ha-onesh*. For *yirat ha-rommemut* [occurs]
when one fears the king out of shame; one is greatly
shamed to draw near to him, due to the king's greatness, for he is a great and awesome king. Because of
this, one loves the king even more, for though the king
is very great and awesome, he still watches over, and
satisfies the needs of, all the residents of his state. One
is simply shamed to draw near to him because of his
greatness and majesty. This is not so with regard to *yirat
ha-onesh*, for this fear distances one from the king. The
distinction is that one fears the king out of [the threat
of] punishment, as one would fear a bear or another
beast; just as the fear of a bear distances one from him—
since [the man] fears for his very life—so too does *yirat
ha-onesh* from God, may He be blessed, distance one
from Him, for one fears to approach Him, lest he be
punished. And now let us return to the verse, "The
counsel of the Lord is with them that fear Him": this
means the treasure of the Holy One, blessed be He,
for the treasure is the counsel. But where is the treasure? "With them that fear Him"; this means that the
men who fear the Holy One, blessed be He, are [them-
selves] His treasure, may He be blessed, for [God's] treasure is fear, as we noted above. "And He will reveal to
them His covenant"; the word *lehodiyam* ("He will
reveal to them") bespeaks interconnection (*hitkashrut*),
such as "And the man knew (*yadah*) Eve" [Gen. 4:1].
This means that [those who fear God] will connect to,
and join with, the Holy One, blessed be He.[1]

This rather lengthy passage yields two important
pieces of information. First, the Maggid's general break-
down of religious fear into two basic types follows the

patterns of those who came before him. Second, the Maggid's interest here relates to the degree to which fear effects the dynamic of interrelationship between God and man. From the outset it is clear that God has a specific desire, or "lack," that only man can fill: God's desire is for man to fear Him. And the nature of that fear is rooted in the notion of shame, a shame that springs from man's self-consciousness in the presence of God's great and awesome personality. The Maggid connects this response to *yirat ha-rommemut*, or the fear of God's majesty.

The experience of shame is so intense that one fears even to draw near to such a God. It would seem, *prima facie*, that this kind of fear would damage, rather than stimulate, any possibility of an intimate relationship between God and man. Yet just the opposite is the case. This higher form of fear is inseparable from love—indeed, it proceeds *from* it. Though God/the king is great and awesome (and thus capable of inspiring fear), he is also the benevolent ruler who "contracts" himself in order to protect and nurture his subjects. This dialectic serves to attract, or "draw in," one who is under his sovereignty; the more one fears God/the king, the more one comes to love him for his gracious, providential care.

The fear that truly distances one from such a figure is *yirat ha-onesh*. In this context, the response of fear relates not to shame (which we have shown promotes a loving relationship) but to actual *revulsion*. Like the man who encounters a bear and moves away from it for fear that it will kill him, so does the subject who fears his king out of the threat of punishment distance himself from his sovereign. It is the desire to avoid pain, rather than the willful act of humility, that results in this lower form of fear. Man fears God because of His power to punish him for his sins, but unless one transcends this level—which even those in the animal kingdom have reached—an intimate relationship between the two will be impossible.

The text makes it plain that man possesses something precious that God wants. The Maggid associates this treasure with the "counsel" (*sod*) of those who fear Him. In this way, they *themselves* become God's treasure, for, as Isaiah 33:6 states, "the fear of the Lord is His treasure." It is to these God-fearers that the Lord will "reveal" His covenant—with the same word, and in the same way, that Adam "knew" (or "revealed himself" to) Eve. The sexual undertones to this phenomenon of revelatory union are clear and common in mystical literature; it is only through the surrender of self that intimate knowledge becomes possible.

Let us digress for a moment on the subject of *yirat ha-onesh*—what it means for man and God. The Maggid writes:

> What is the meaning of [the verse], "What does the Lord thy God require of thee, but to fear the Lord thy God?" [Deu. 10:12]. "To fear the Lord thy God" means that one's fear should be like God's fear, for simple human fear is *yirat ha-onesh*, which is nothing. But the fear God has for man is *yirat ha-het* (the fear of sin), in that the Holy One, blessed be He, perpetually fears, as it were, that man will sin, out of His great compassion for him. This is analogous to a father who perpetually fears for his son, lest he stray into licentiousness (*tarbut ra'ah*), or fall ill. . . .[2]

The Maggid claims that man's fear of God (here called "the fear of sin") should mirror God's fear for him. The fear God feels for man is moored in love and compassion; He fears for his creature's well-being, as a father fears for the health of his son. The Maggid goes on to demonstrate that the human inability to commonly reach beyond *yirat ha-onesh* is a consequence of the issue of perspective:

> This situation is like the father who warns his son not to go outside barefoot, lest he step on a thorn, while the young boy—who still lacks understanding—does not heed [his warning] and goes outside barefoot [anyway], and has a thorn enter his foot. Though the pain from [the thorn] is not great, the father fears that it may cause his son's foot to swell. What does the father do? He takes an awl and tears the skin around the thorn and removes the thorn from his [son's] foot. Even though this [tearing causes] the child great pain, and though he screams bitterly, the father knows that this pain is [that which will] heal him, and he ignores the cries of the child and forcefully removes the thorn. . . . For the child's distress was rooted in the removal of the thorn. . .while the father was not fearful or worried about its removal, since, on the contrary, he knew that it would heal him. Thus we see that the fear of the father and [the fear of] the son are not equivalent. . . . [So too] are the fear of God and [the fear of] man not equivalent, for man fears only punishment, and not the sin itself, while God, as it were, fears and worries that man will sin. [God] does not fear the punishment that man [will receive] after his sin, since, on the contrary, this is God's compassion and healing, for He punishes [man] in order to purify him from his sins. This explains "What does the Lord thy God require of thee, but to fear the Lord thy God" [Deu. 10:12]: let your fear be like His fear, as we mentioned above.[3]

What from the divine perspective is providential care is, from the human standpoint, unbearable suffering. Only he who truly fears will understand this and be moved to love God for His compassion. The Maggid explains this position through the use of an analogy: a child, ignoring the warnings of his loving father, goes outside barefoot and steps on a thorn. Though removing the thorn will hurt the child more than the presence of the thorn itself, the father (who has superior knowledge and foresight) removes it from his foot and pays no heed to his cries, understanding that whatever pain the child feels now is nothing compared to the dangers of a likely infection later.

Their two fears are not the same. The father fears for his son's overall health and well-being, while the child fears only the pain of the thorn's removal. The irony is this: the child, due to his inferior understanding, fears the very thing that will help him. As the Maggid writes elsewhere, "the child does not fear the damage, but rather the healing, that is, the removal of the thorn."[4] The absence of immediate harm deludes the child into thinking that all is well. He cannot understand the "tough love" of his father, which allows him to inflict pain on his son for the sake of a later benefit.

This story helps to explain the relationship of God to man, as well as the concept of *yirat ha-onesh*. With regard to sinful behavior, man fears not the sin itself but the punishment that God will inflict upon him in recompense. The sin, like the thorn, may not cause the man much pain now but, as the thorn infects the child's body, so will the sin corrupt the man's soul. As the father removes the thorn to heal his son, so does God punish the man in order to purify him from his sins. God fears that man will sin, not the punishment he will receive for it, since this punishment is merely an expression of God's love for him (in much the same way that external fears are the manifestations of God's love for man in Yaakov Yosef's system). It is man's task to transform *yirat ha-onesh* into *yirat ha-het* and thus attain the divine perspective—the true vision of reality.

We have seen how Yaakov Yosef moves beyond the two classical rubrics for fear and creates his own subcategories of the response. The Maggid does the same. He writes:

> "The eyes of the Lord are upon the zaddikim" (Ps. 34:16); [this means] that there are three [types of] fear: the fear of punishment (*yirat ha-onesh*), the fear of the Creator's greatness (*yirat gedulat ha-Borey*), and the fear of shame (*yirat ha-bushah*). [The fear of shame occurs] when one knows by himself that he is absolutely nothing compared to his Creator. The fear of the Creator's greatness is below the love of the Creator; the fear of shame, however, is above love. These are the two higher fears. They are [God's] eyes: the fear of [God's] greatness is the left eye, [or] external fear; the fear of shame, [which is] internal fear, is the right eye. Thus, "The eyes of the Lord" [describes] two eyes; "are upon the zaddikim" [means] that the zaddikim possess the two fears mentioned above. But "The eye of the Lord is upon those who fear Him" (Ps. 33:18) means that [those who fear God] do not possess external fear [but rather internal fear alone]. Therefore, *eyin* is the one [and supreme] eye. This is hinted at in the Zohar (I: 11b), [which associates the word] *bereyshit* ("In the beginning") [with the commandment to fear God, which it considers the first commandment]. This is the fear of shame, which is internal fear and [God's] right eye.[5]

This passage is not concerned with the lower form of fear (*yirat ha-onesh*); instead, it focuses only on the two higher categories: the fear of the Creator's greatness and the fear of shame. (Two other fears in the Maggid's system—the fear of sin and the fear of God's majesty—are not mentioned here by name.) The fear of shame, as we have seen previously, is the self-consciousness of one's own nothingness compared to God. The fear of God's greatness is not defined here, though it seems to imply the cognizance of God's greatness *without* the awareness of one's existential insignificance.

The Maggid calls these responses the two higher fears, though there is a difference in value between them: *yirat gedulat ha-Borey*, or the fear of God's greatness, lies below the love of God, whereas *yirat ha-bushah*, or the fear of shame, is above it. From a theosophical perspective, this latter fear represents the sphere of *hokhmah*, which becomes clear at the end of the text. These two fears parallel God's two eyes. The fear of God's greatness, as another form of external fear (and thus a notch higher than the lowly *yirat ha-onesh*), is His left eye; the fear of shame, which is internal fear, represents God's right eye. The zaddikim possess both of these fears, while the "God-fearers," having jettisoned the inferior external type, possess internal fear, and that alone.[6]

There are two reasons we should connect the fear of shame with the sphere of wisdom. First, the Maggid calls it God's "right" eye, and *hokhmah* is in the upper right corner of the sefirotic tree, just below *arikh anpin*. Second, he alludes to the Zohar's association of fear with wisdom. Yet the Maggid unites wisdom with a particular kind of fear, the fear of shame. In a standard hasidic wordplay, he supports this claim through the juxtaposition of the letters of *bereyshit* with those of *yerey boshet*. That the concept of nothingness—an integral feature of the fear of shame—is also joined to the notion of *hokh-mah* will be taken up in the next chapter.

The Maggid utilizes the phrase *yirah penimiyut*, or "internal fear," as a kind of catchall designation for the triad of names that come to constitute this highest level of religious fear. He seems to conflate the fear of shame (by way of association) with two other more familiar names for the true fear of God:

> [With regard to the commandment to fear God,] the Torah does not refer to external fear, for this is [merely] the fear of punishment. To attain this fear, there is no need at all for wisdom, since even those with little intelligence are able to achieve it. . . . The fear of sin, however, is [on] a high and exalted level. In this case, one fears the sin itself, whereas the fear we mentioned previously is [only] the fear of punishment, and not of the sin itself. The fear about which we are speaking here, however, is *yirat ha-rommemut* (the fear of God's majesty), which is called *yirah penimiyut* (internal fear), and which is really *yirat het* (the fear of sin). This means that one fears the sin itself, because it opposes the might of [God's] majesty, may He be blessed. In order to achieve this fear, one truly needs great wisdom and limitless strength.[7]

Earlier in this chapter, we saw how the fear of God's majesty was connected with the experience of shame; here it is connected with the cognizance of sin. To fear punishment for one's sin is nothing, but to fear the sin *itself*—as we observed in the parable of the thorn—is to elevate oneself to the divine perspective. This, truly, is *yirat ha-rommemut*, and explains the injunction to

"let your fear be like [God's] fear."[8] The rationale behind the fear of sin is simple: each act of sin is an act of
opposition to God's majesty, or *rommemut*. (Interest-
ingly, the Maggid is not here concerned with opposition to God's *will*, but to His *majesty*; it is not the moral
plane to which the fear of sin refers, but rather to the
spiritual one.) The fear of shame, the fear of sin, and
the fear of God's majesty all share certain common features: an identification with internal fear, an association
with wisdom, and a similarity in phenominal behavior.
In this way, they must be seen as merely different names
for a single phenomenon—the elevation of the human
soul to the divine plane.

What is the process through which this dynamic
occurs? The Maggid explains:

> External fear [takes place] when, due to fear, all [one's]
> powers and attributes disappear and become as noth-
> ing. But internal fear takes place thereafter, when one
> has become nothing (*ayin*) and the supernal forces and
> attributes dwell upon him, and then there rests upon
> him the [feeling] of shame—this is the essence of life,
> when the supernal attributes dwell upon him.[9]

The most basic of fears is little more than the pri-
mal reaction to God's greatness, an experience which
carries with it the potential to shatter all of one's cognitive and psychic structures—an event and effect akin
to the human confrontation with a tiger or a bear. All
that is left in such a situation is the (potentially paralyz-
ing) emotional response of terror. After this stage, however, one may reach the level of internal fear, where
one is actually transformed into *ayin*, or nothing. As a
result, "the supernal forces and attributes" surface within
him, accompanied by the feeling of shame. Shame,

therefore, does not mark a revulsion from, but rather a recognition of, the presence of divinity within oneself— which, for the Maggid, constitutes the "essence" of life. He continues:

> The second level [of fear] is called shame (*bushah*), that is, [when one knows] that his powers and attributes come from the supernal levels and attributes and thereafter dwell in him, and that all his powers are nothing. And this is the essence of his vitality: that his levels become as nothing, and his roots dwell upon him. This explains [the phrase,] "He who wishes to live, must put himself to death."[10]

Once the mystic understands that all his human *potentia* ultimately derive from a supernal source (and thus, in themselves, are "nothing"), he becomes filled with fear. As a consequence, his own levels shed their illusory skins. In their nothingness, a space is made in which the supernal roots may now dwell. It is this indwelling of the divine element that is the foundation of the mystic's shame. While the human *potentia* disintegrate—or reveal their true nothingness—the supernal "roots" become activated and enlivened. Unlike Yaakov Yosef, for whom internal fear leads to the negation of external fears, the Maggid presents a rather different picture: for him, internal fear, or the fear of shame, leads to the negation of one's very sense of *self.*

In the Maggid's system, the supernal power that operates within the mystic has a specific personality— the *Shekhinah.* He writes:

> When one reflects before prayer [on] what he will say, and before whom he will say [it], fear and shame will surely descend upon him, for he will fear the words

themselves. When he acknowledges that the World of Speech is the *Shekhinah*, as it were, speaking within him, and [that the *Shekhinah*] draws in all of the attributes—love, fear, *tiferet*, and all the rest—how could he *not* fear and be shamed that the *Shekhinah*, and all the [other] attributes, had become aroused?[11]

When one contemplates the letters of prayer (or the "vessels" designed to contain the divine influx) and realizes before whom one will utter them (the *Shekhinah*, or *malkhut*, the gateway to the sefirotic world), he will become filled with fear and shame. For the Maggid, "the World of Speech is the World of Fear,"[12] and it is in this space that the *Shekhinah* contracts itself and resides. As the last sefirah, it is the *Shekhinah* which receives the influx of all of the higher emanations, and it is the *Shekhinah*, as it becomes internalized through prayer, which speaks via the mystic. The presence of this immanent reality within him is the cause of the mystic's fear.

It is the *Shekhinah* within the mystic that strives to unite itself with God:

> When a man studies or prays, the word should be uttered with full strength, like the ejaculation of a drop of semen from his whole body, when his [whole] strength is "dressed" (*melubash*) within that [one] drop. In the same way, his whole strength should be "dressed" within the word [of prayer]. . . . His strength is the soul (*neshamah*) that spreads throughout [his] body, and the soul is part of God above; this is true adhesion (*devekut*), [when] the part [unites with] its root, for the souls of the zaddikim are the limbs of the *Shekhinah*, as it were. This is the union of the Holy One, blessed

be He, and the *Shekhinah*, which explains [the verse] "What does the Lord (YHWH) thy God (*elohekhah*) require of thee, but to fear the Lord thy God" [Deu. 10:12]; this means [the union] of YHWH, who is the Holy One, blessed be He, and *elohekhah*, which is "your strength," or the *Shekhinah*.[13]

The unification of God with His *Shekhinah*—or the feminine, divine power immanent in man—is interpreted here not as a metaphysical process within the Godhead, but rather as the union of God with the soul of man. When the *Shekhinah* is activated within the mystic, then he himself becomes the host, or one of the "limbs," of the *Shekhinah* itself. Only then is it possible for the human soul to achieve a state of union (*yikhud*) with its Root, or God. The obvious sexual imagery hearkens back to the notion of *hitkashrut* (interconnection) between Adam and Eve noted at the outset of this chapter as a metaphor for describing the revelatory encounter between God and man.

The Maggid dispels any suggestion that adhesion to God is possible without the attribute of fear. He writes that

> . . . fear is born as a result of adhesion. Just as fear is born in the slave [out of his relationship] with his master, so is the *Shekhinah* [born] in us through divine revelation. Love without fear is [like] wasted seed, and this is what fell as a consequence of the Breaking [of the Vessels].[14]

This passage is coherent only after one understands the identity between the *Shekhinah* and fear.[15] The attainment of a relationship with God itself gives "birth" to (or activates) the *Shekhinah* within the mystic. Since the fear of God is identical with the *Shekhinah*, it is impossible to reach the state of *devekut* without it. The love of God alone is not sufficient: it is like wasted seed, a shell from the shattered cosmos that only the fear of God can make whole once again.[16]

3

Brushes with the Void

The Maggid makes it plain that fear is the result of the moment of contact between the human and the divine. In the previous chapter we demonstrated that the experience of *ayin*, or nothingness, punctuates such an encounter. It is the mystic's reduction to *ayin* which allows the space for the activation of the *Shekhinah*, which in turn makes a union between the finite and infinity possible. It is the purpose of this chapter to explore this notion of *ayin*, along with its other associated spiritual phenomena.

Our author writes that "When [a man] has arrived at the level of [internal] fear, he thinks of himself as *ayin*."[1] In other words, internal fear is associated with a negative self-consciousness: the mystic considers himself as if he is "not," or as if he has no true existence. Schatz-Uffenheimer writes that "this fact is the prerequisite that provides the man [with] the mystical ability to reach the divine Nothing, which is [the sefirah of] *hokhmah*."[2] It would seem that fear is, paradoxically, both the cause and the result of the condition of *ayin*. The Maggid corroborates this strange dialectic in another text:

> Because of the power of the attribute of fear, one arrives at the attribute of Nothing (*ayin*), which is called wisdom (*hokhmah*), as it is written, "From where (*mey'ayin*) shall wisdom be found?" [Job 28:12]; and [from this] one obviously reaches true life.[3]

The pun on the word *ayin* allows the Maggid to connect wisdom with the state of nothingness. Since, as we have shown, internal fear corresponds to the sefirah of *hokhmah* (wisdom), then it is clear from the above passage how the attribute of fear serves a dialectical purpose with regard to the passage from *ayin* to the "true life," or *unio mystica*. Though fear leads to the state of *ayin*, it is also identified with it: the Maggid writes that "*shame* leads to *ayin*, which is the fear of God."[4] He goes on to explain how one enters the gate of *ayin*:

> One must think of oneself as *ayin* and forget oneself totally. . . . Then one can transcend time, rising to the World of Thought, where all is equal: life and death, ocean and dry land. . . . Such is not the case when one is attached to the corporeal nature of this world. . . . If one thinks of oneself as something (*yesh*) . . . then the Holy One, blessed be He, cannot clothe Himself in him, for He is Eyn Sof (infinity), and no vessel can withstand Him, unless one thinks of oneself as *ayin*.[5]

Because God's nature is infinite and incorporeal, man can only make the space in which He may enter if he *himself* transcends the material world. To consider oneself as *yesh*—or "something"—is to think of oneself as a substantial being; yet a material vessel cannot contain that which is essentially immaterial. To make room for Eyn Sof, the mystic must "forget" himself or think of himself as nothing. As we have discussed, the progression from fear to shame is the process that enables the mystic to reach the state of *ayin*, where he contracts himself and provides the emptiness in which God can dwell. Moses, yet again, is the paradigm for this ascent toward the encounter with infinity:

> Among the zaddikim themselves we find a distinction [with regard to spiritual merit]: Abraham said "I am but dust and ashes" [Gen. 18:27], and David said "I am a worm, and no man" [Ps. 22:7]—these men both [still claim] a degree of existence. But Moses asked "What are we?" [Ex. 16:7]; [this means that] he was in a state of *ayin*, as it is written, "Now the man Moses was very humble, more so than all the men who were upon the face of the earth" [Nu. 12:3]. He therefore understood the divine essence (*etzem*), which is not the case with the rest of the prophets who came before or after him. In this way, the more a prophet cleaved to fear, which is wisdom, the more he [increased] his understanding [of God's true essence].[6]

Though masters of humility, both Abraham and David still retain a sense of self-consciousness, albeit a negative one. Moses, on the other hand, questions the very *fact* of his existence or material reality. His words demonstrate that he did not consider himself to be even dust. Fear, equated with wisdom, seems to be the sword that slays one's sense of self and brings one to the level of nothingness. For the Maggid, "*ayin* is the only state of mind appropriate for one who seeks to become a divine vessel"[7]; as a consequence of his attainment of this state, Moses—and he alone—is able to become filled with, and fully grasp, the divine essence.

In another passage, the Maggid places fear on an even higher level than *ayin* and appears to connect it with *unio mystica* itself:

> "What (*mah*) does the Lord thy God require of thee, but to fear the Lord thy God?" [Deu. 10:12]; this implies the level of *ayin*, and means that one should vigorously engage in the contemplation [of God's greatness and majesty] . . . until he arrives at the level of *ayin*, through which mankind has been chosen to praise God. . . . Thus [Moses] and his brothers asked, "What (*mah*) are we?" [Ex. 16:7]; this implies [the level of] *ayin*, and means that God wants us to strive to reach the levels of *mah* and *ayin*. [The first verse further states] that God requires this [effort] through "fear," which means that after one arrives at the level of *mah*, which is *ayin*, shame and fear will come to him—the fear of God's majesty, or the fear of sin, which is the peak of the supernal levels.[8]

In this text the Maggid connects the word *mah* with that of *ayin*. When one asks the existential question "What am I?" it serves as the proof that one has reached the level of nothingness, the place where self-consciousness collapses. In the wake of this disintegration of identity, the mystic is infused with shame and fear. It is this fear—*yirat ha-rommemut* or *yirat ha-het*—which becomes identified with the summit of the sefirotic ladder, above even the level of *ayin/hokhmah*. All that is left is *keter*, and at this level one is brought into contact with the very wellspring of the divine emanations. Here the mystic may grasp "the branches of the supernal levels, and ascend the ladder to wisdom, and to the fear and shame that come from it, and merit [the vision] to behold God's beauty."[9] The fear of God leads directly to the vision of God, to *unio mystica*.

The Maggid has a technical name for the annihilation of self-consciousness: *bitul mi-metziut*. Though this concept overlaps the notion of *ayin*,[10] it is critical to examine its specific phenomenological effects if one is to fully understand the Maggid's views on the mystical encounter. The Maggid returns to the image of the king in order to describe the idea of self-annihilation and how it relates to the mystic's confrontation with God:

> If one of the king's ministers stands before him, and an object which he [normally] desires passes in front of him, . . . he will not desire it because he is in the king's presence. This occurs due to the great shame and fear he feels because of the king, [and lasts] until he no longer has any sense of himself, since all [the minsters] are negated from existence because of [their] fear of the king. Thus the rabbis write, "To what may one compare a zaddik before God? [To] a candle before a torch" [BT Pesakhim 8a]; just as [this candle] is useless and unable to function, so are the attributes [of the zaddikim] unable to function [in relation to] worldly desires, for they are perpetually negated from existence before God. Now fear is a level beneath the king, since the king himself has no fear, . . . and it is that which joins the king to his people.[11]

For a minister to be in the presence of a king is sufficient enough force to negate not only his desires but also his very sense of self. The fear he experiences by his master's presence nullifies all his other loves, fears, hatreds, lusts—in other words, those qualities that constitute the fabric of his individual personality. With regard to the zaddik/mystic before God, the same phenomenon of *bitul mi-metziut* applies. As the self is annihilated in the mystical encounter, both desire and identity dissipate. Fear is the cause of self-annihilation as well as the connective tissue between God and the mystic and the king and his subjects. While Yaakov Yosef uses the zaddik as the medium between God and the masses, the Maggid transforms fear itself into the unifier of opposites.

None of this can occur as long as one remains attached to corporeality. It is the mystic's abnegation of the mortal "form"—i.e., his existence as a human being—that allows for the attainment of his true, *ideal* form:

> "Make thee two trumpets (*hatzotzrot*) of silver" [Nu. 10:2]; that is, two half-forms (*hatzi tzurot*), as in "And upon the likeness of the throne was the likeness as the appearance of a man above upon it" [Ez. 1:26], for man is only *dalet mem* [i.e., *dam*, or "blood"—the last two letters of the word *adam*], and speech inheres in him. But when he adheres to the Holy One, blessed be He, who is the Master of the World (*Alufo shel Olam*) [i.e., the *Alef* of the world], he becomes man (*Adam*) . . . and a man must separate himself from all corporeality, so that he ascends via all the worlds and unites with the Holy One, blessed be He, until he himself is negated from existence; then he may be called *Adam*.[12]

When the half-form of flesh ("blood") cleaves to the half-form of spirit (*Alef*), the product is the ideal man—the mystic. The detachment from corporeality is the prerequisite of this metamorphosis. As the mystic separates himself from the material world, he is able to penetrate the world of the spirit and ascend it to the

point of unity with God. At that moment he is negated
from existence, i.e., his sense of self is annihilated. As
Idel comments, "the reference to union as a step preceding annihilation is evidence that the unitive experience culminates with the total loss of individuality."[13]
For the Maggid, it is not *devekut* that marks the climax
of the spiritual quest, but *bitul mi-metziut*. If the concept of *ayin* is the assumption that the world itself has
no real existence apart from God, then the notion of
self-annihilation is the *consciousness* of that fundamental
nothingness.

At the moment of *unio mystica*, all activities apart
from thought cease to function; the mystic then "may
become spiritualized and enjoy a new dimension of
spiritual existence."[14] The final consequence of the transcendence of corporeality is an elevation of the spirit
to a brush with the *mysterium tremendum*. The Maggid
writes:

> This is what is stated in *Pirkei Heikhalot*: that when the
> Holy One, blessed be He, is sitting upon the throne,
> there descends upon the creatures (*hayot*) a silent fire;
> that is, when the Holy One dwells upon the words,
> there descends upon the vitality (*hayut*) of the man a
> fire of silence, that is, a great fear. . . . Thus fear falls
> upon him, and he does not know where he is, nor
> does he see or hear, for the power of the corporeal is
> negated. And this is the meaning of "Happy is the king
> who is thus praised in his house" [BT Berakhot 3a]—
> that the body becomes the house of the Holy One,
> blessed be He, for he must pray with all his strength
> until he bursts out of corporeality and forgets his own
> self, so that only the vitality that is in God remains, and
> all his thoughts are directed to Him. [In this state of
> orison] he will not even be aware of the intensity of

his prayer, for if he is he will remember himself. And all this occurs in one moment, in a flash, so that we see that he has transcended time [itself].[15]

This description of the phenomenological features of *unio mystica* highlights several aspects of the Maggid's spiritual system and the role of fear within it. When God "sits on the throne"—i.e., when the *Shekhinah* irrupts inside a man's soul—the mystic experiences the descent of a "silent fire." The *Shekhinah*, as we have discussed, is equated with fear, and thus so is the silent fire. This fear is the direct cause of the mystic's negation from existence: in his psychic disorientation, he loses touch with his own senses and then "forgets" his very self. The Maggid explains this phenomenon elsewhere:

The true fear is that which falls upon a man [and makes him] shake and tremble, and because of [this fear] he does not know where he is. Yet the mind is purified [through this experience], and tears fall from [the man's] eyes.[16]

The violence of the ontic assault can generate external manifestations: in the throes of the ecstatic experience, the mystic's body may shake and tremble. The disorientation, though terrifying, is also the cause for celebration, since this "trial by fire" leads to the purification of the mystic's mind/consciousness. As the mystic's sense of self is annihilated, so is the illusion that he and the world have independent realities apart from God. With a purified mind, he now directs all his thoughts to God, so much so that he loses the awareness of even his own intensity—for each thought of the self is a consciousness of the self. This brush with divinity and one's own self-destruction takes place like a "flash," without duration. The divine encounter lifts the mystic above all aspects of corporeality: the world, the self, and even time.

Paul Tillich writes that "there is no revelation without ecstasy."[17] The experience of ecstasy, the state in which the mind transcends its ordinary situation and structures, does not necessarily entail outwardly visible manifestations:

> Sometimes a man is able to pray in love, fear, and great enthusiasm without any [external] movement. . . . [In this condition] he may serve God with his soul alone, . . . which is better service, and more effective to adhere to God, may He be blessed, than the prayer that is visible externally through his limbs.[18]

Once the mystic has reached the higher levels of meditation and prayer, it matters little whether he speaks or is silent (though the latter is the favored mode of expression). If he speaks, it is automatic speech, or the *Shekhinah* speaking through him; if he is silent, he serves God through his soul alone, and the only movement is the motion of his thoughts. Elsewhere the Maggid writes that nonverbal prayer is, in fact, the proper way to respond to the "fire of silence" that burns within the mystic. As a result of its presence, he will "cry out in silence" from the passion to serve his God.[19] Though there is no exterior sign, an entire world of spiritual activity is taking place within the mystic's soul. On this point, we may draw upon the image of Kierkegaard's knight of faith, about whom he claims that "if one did not know him, it would be impossible to distinguish him from the rest of the crowd, . . . and yet this man has made and at every moment is making the movement of infinity."[20]

The comparison of *unio mystica* with fire is common in the Maggid's homilies and has antecedents as far back as the Torah.[21] The Maggid writes:

> "For the Lord thy God is a consuming fire (*eish okhlah*)" [Deu. 4:24]; this describes the fire and the enthusiasm from the zaddik below. This is [what God] eats (*akhilah*), and [what] maintains [Him] above. Thus "a consuming fire" refers to the [zaddik's] enthusiasm, which is called "a fiery serpent."[22]

This unusual passage combines two classical notions related to *unio mystica*. It retains the standard mystical metaphor of "swallowing," whereby the divine soul consumes its human counterpart in order to elevate it.[23] Yet it reverses the traditional conception of God as a "devouring fire" and, instead, connects the image of fire with the figure of the zaddik/mystic himself. In this dialectic, the mystic provides the spiritual sustenance for God while at the same time being elevated as a consequence of his own consumption by God. The Maggid presents additional evidence for the joining of fire to the brush with God:

> Is it possible to make oneself adhere to the Holy One, blessed be He? For [God] is "a consuming fire" [Deu. 4:24]; rather, one should adhere to His attributes. . . . To serve God with enthusiasm—which is true *devekut*— is impossible on a constant basis, but only temporarily [*matei ve'lo matei*, which literally means "it touches but does not touch"], like the behavior of fire. One may extinguish a newly-lit fire by blowing on it; after it has

grown into a pyre, however, the flames ascend and descend, flickering [on and off]. Similarly, enthusiasm [*hitlahavut*, whose root word is *lahav*, or "flame"] is temporary, for a constant pleasure (*ta'anug*) is no pleasure. . . . Enthusiasm keeps one back from [God, who is the] "consuming fire"; thus it becomes possible to adhere to Him, may He be blessed.[24]

If God is like fire, is it possible for the mystic to cleave to Him? Since God's essence, like a flame, is intangible, then the mystic must adhere to those aspects of God which *are* tangible—and these are His attributes. True adhesion to God Himself is impossible as a permanent state but may be experienced as a temporary "brush." Just as a pyre flickers in and out of existence, so does the enthusiasm that mediates between God and man: one may "touch and not touch" God. It is just this boundary, however, that protects the mystic from the violence of the consuming fire and makes the encounter with infinity more akin to a brush than to an actual merger.[25]

In the above two passages, the mystic's enthusiasm is described as both the "food" and the "pleasure" of God (though, as we saw in chapter one, if either is constant, it loses its value). Schatz-Uffenheimer writes that pleasure, or *ta'anug*, is the happiness that derives "from the meeting between the divine element within man and the Godhead which is outside of him."[26] Yet the Maggid suggests that this pleasure belongs to God as well as to the mystic. He writes:

When a zaddik serves the Holy One, blessed be He, he brings a great pleasure to the world. As he himself becomes aroused [from the pleasure], so does it cause arousal in the Holy One, blessed be He.[27]

The experience of *ta'anug* is a twofold one: just as the mystic derives pleasure from his encounter with God, so does God derive pleasure from the mystic's actions. Thus God is able to treat the mystic as His pleasure, or spiritual nourishment, while simultaneously allowing for the mystic to experience a pleasure of his own. We have discussed how the *Shekhinah* is identified with internal fear. The Maggid explains how this fear is itself the supreme pleasure of the Holy One:

> The foundation of kingship is fear, for the root of the king's pleasure is that [his subjects] will fear him—and through this they will obey him. Thus God made [man in such a way] that he would fear Him, and the essence of the world's creation was for the sake of this pleasure, which is called "bride." We are connected to this [bride], to be forever married to the fear of God, may He be blessed. This [fear] exists whenever the *Shekhinah* is revealed within us, that is, the pleasure of the fear of God, which is always within us.[28]

Just as a mortal kingdom is founded on the principle of fear, so is God's world—and it was for the sake of this fear that the world was created. Like a bride, the fear of God is joined to every man *in potentia*, as a permanent (yet hidden) fixture in his psychic structure. The bride is the *Shekhinah*, and it is the common possession—and pleasure—of both God and man, once it has become manifest through *unio mystica*.

Following the pattern of Yaakov Yosef, the Maggid uses the story of the Exodus as a paradigm for the phenomenon of the mystical encounter. He writes:

> The goal is that, prior to prayer, [the mystic] should cast off corporeality, which is finite, and enter into the

attribute of Nothing, which is infinite. A man ought to direct all of his attention towards the Creator alone, and not to any thing—or [even] half a thing—of his own being, which is impossible unless he brings himself within the attribute of Nothing; that is, that he does not exist at all, and he then may not turn to any thing of this world, since he does not exist at all, but let man rely only upon his Maker, upon God alone. Understand this. This attribute of casting off corporeality is a redemption of the [vital] soul of man, [and] of his spirit and soul which are redeemed from the corporeality of the body, which is confined and limited and narrow (*metzarim*), and [they] cleave to the Creator, who is Eyn Sof (infinite). And this is called the Redemption from Egypt (*Mitzrayim*). This is the reason for joining Redemption to Prayer [i.e., linking the end of the *Shema* to the *Amidah* in the morning service]. . . . Thus, "O Lord, open my lips" [Ps. 51:17] means that . . . You shall open the fetters and chains of corporeality, to cast them off me, that I may be attached to the Nothing.[29]

The precondition for entrance into the divine *ayin* is the transcendence of the corporeal world: the mystical "possibilities opened to a person depend upon the breaking of the bonds of limited matter."[30] As the consequence of spiritual concentration directed entirely toward the Creator, God Himself rescues man and frees him completely from the bonds of finitude. Prayer, which begins with the mystic's activity, ultimately transforms into an act of pure passivity. As the mystic disintegrates into *ayin*, he becomes filled with the divine infinity— the force that redeems his soul from the bonds of limited being (or perhaps even from being itself). This is the Redemption from Egypt. It is not, as Yaakov Yosef argues, the negation of worldly fears, but rather the negation of the world *itself*, with all that entails. One of those entailments is the negation of a conception of self; another is the annihilation of thought:

> Every day we arouse the Redemption from Egypt: for by means of the letters [of prayer], we are able to attach our vitality [to God]. And we must first remove the vitality from our corporeal thoughts and from our own being: that is, so that we may enter the gate of the Nothing, and we are then easily able to be attached by our root to the Cause of all Causes. And this is the matter of the Redemption from Egypt: while our intellect is still [concerned with] the matter of our selves and is within the gate of being, the intelligibles are contracted and narrowed; but when one comes to the root, they are in a state of expansion [towards infinity].[31]

As long as the human mind is capable of reflecting upon itself, it cannot reach the divine Nothing. Only through the extinction of the "reflective consciousness" will it be possible for the mystic to become liberated from the *yesh*, or being. After its entrance into the Nothing, the limited mind acquires a new capacity for infinity; it enlarges and expands, thus allowing for the absorption of aspects of the divine mind. The Redemption from Egypt releases the intellect from its finitude in the "gate of being"; it lifts it above its ontic situation into the realm of the Nothing, the world of pure spiritual consciousness.

For the Maggid, Moses is the embodiment of the expanded intellect:

> Moses is called the Intellect, for man has the power to escape from that intellect to another intellect, and to come to the threshold of the Nothing. And Moses is

named for the language of "removal," as in, "from the water he was drawn" [Ex. 2:10]. For he leaves his [own] mind and goes into the border of the Nothing, and this is, "Suffer [*katar*, a play on *keter*] me a little, and I will show thee" [Job 36:2], for he needs to enter into the limit of the Nothing, to leave the Intellect and Knowledge and go into the boundary of the Nothing, and afterwards, "From Nothing (*mey'ayin*) is wisdom found" [Job 28:12].[32]

The figure of Moses depicted above serves as a paradigm for the ecstatic mystic, in that he is able to transcend (or "escape from") ordinary consciousness. Moses literally "goes out of his mind" and reaches the threshold of *ayin*—the place where thought ends and Nothing begins. This moment of liminality—the brush of the human mind against the abyss of infinity—gives birth to wisdom, which is identified with mystical fear. In the Maggid's system, spiritual transformation can come about only by one's passing through nothingness, and no one can pass through nothingness without the experience of utter fear.

4

Life After Death

In Yaakov Yosef's system, the redemption of the self functions as the ultimate goal of the fear of God. The Maggid, however, makes it clear that, for him, the fear of God is instead associated with the *annihilation* of the self. Yet what occurs in the aftermath of the death of self-consciousness? This last chapter will address the end result of *unio mystica*, i.e., that which follows the brush with infinity and the destruction of identity. It is the thesis of this chapter that, though the mystical encounter leads to "death," it also leads to new life, new being, and spiritual transformation.

The Maggid writes that the quality of *ayin* makes possible the union of opposites:

> That which one loves, one cannot fear, and that which one fears, one cannot love. But when these [opposite responses] relate to God, may He be blessed, they [form] a single unity—for the quality of *ayin* unites everything. It is impossible to reach the level of wisdom until one

has reached the attribute of fear, for there is no wisdom without fear. Thus, when one truly fears the Creator, it is obvious that he will [also] love [Him].[1]

According to the Maggid, one cannot both fear and love objects of the corporeal world simultaneously. When the referent of these responses is God Himself, however, such a duality does indeed become possible. This results from the fact that the divine Nothing (equated with wisdom and proceeding fear) serves as the mediating force for the union of opposites.[2] He who is rooted in corporeality cannot transcend the existential state of "division" (*either* one fears *x, or* one loves *x*). The mystic, however, is able to reach the level of *ayin*, and in this mode all divisions are negated. The Maggid goes on:

> [With regard to] divine service, there is love and there is fear, and each opposes the other. How, then, is it possible for both to exist together? If, for instance, one fears a snake, there is no love present in this fear; or, similarly, with regard to a good thing, one has only love for it [without any presence of fear]. If, however, one loves or fears the Creator, it is possible for both to exist as one. And love is called "day," and fear is called "night," and that which unites them is called "twilight."[3]

The Maggid rejects an admixture of emotions relating to corporeal referents: if one fears a snake, there is no room in that response for the presence of love. Each response, whether it be fear or love, must be pure and unmediated by any other kind of response. When these two attributes are directed toward God, however, a union between them may now exist. The metaphor of twilight explains this apparent paradox: just as twilight unites day and night without being either itself, so does *ayin* unite love and fear. The Maggid does not make it clear why this dynamic applies only to the supernal realm, though he illustrates this process through a homily on the Akedah:

> "And behold behind him a ram" [Gen. 22:13]: the Zohar comments that "this is the ram that was created at twilight,[4] and was one year old" [Zohar I: 120b]; the meaning of "twilight" is the middle thing between day and night. In every thing there are four foundations: fire, water, wind, and earth. All of these things oppose one another—water extinguishes fire, wind scatters earth. It is necessary for there to be an additional [thing] which unites them, and this is the attribute of *ayin*. For when the foundation of water negates the foundation of fire, it [itself] is negated from existence, as it arrives at the attribute of *ayin*. The same applies to love and fear: if one loves a corporeal thing, then he cannot fear it at the same time, and if he fears it, he cannot love it. With regard to God, however, love and fear can be present as one, for [God] unites them. . . . *Ayin* is called "wisdom," since "From *ayin* is wisdom found" [Job 28:12]. And wisdom is [called] "beginning," [for] "The beginning of wisdom is the fear of the Lord" [Ps. 111:10]. . . . Day is called "light" (*behirut*), since man sees the light of God, may He be blessed, and night is called "darkness," since he is not able to see His light. That which unites the two is *ayin*. This is "twilight"—the middle thing between day and night. And this was the matter of the Akedah, for [Abraham tried] to lift up Isaac [who is representative of fear] to the attribute of love, . . . and he certainly needed to elevate him through the attribute of *ayin*. "And [the ram] was one year old (*u'ven shanah haya*)"—*shanah* is the language of transformation (*shi-*

nui), that is, through [*ayin*] one may transform [oneself],
as it is written, "The Lord by wisdom founded the earth"
[Prov. 3:19]. God, may He be blessed, dwells in wisdom, though wisdom is a level below Him, may He
be blessed. It is an emanation from Him, His initial
thought.[5]

For the Maggid, the world is made up of four dis-
parate and oppositional elements, and it is only through
the mediation of *ayin* that a unified, functional existence is made possible. At the moment of transition from
one state to another, nothingness becomes manifest. As
the ontic realities of water and fire collide, a double
negation takes place: water negates the existence of fire
and, though just for an instant, fire negates the existence of water. This results from the fact that, at the
moment of *ayin*, both elements lose their full sense of
identity—the product of such a collision, at the *instant*
of its violence, is neither water nor fire. It is nothing.
    A similar dynamic occurs with regard to human
emotions. As we have noted, as long as the referent of
one's love or fear is rooted in corporeality, one cannot both love it *and* fear it simultaneously. If the referent is God, however, then love and fear may coexist;
though the result of divine unification, both responses
retain the integrity of their respective identities. As
twilight connects the day with the night, so does *ayin*
form the link between love and fear: it is the psychological moment of passage from the vision of God's
light to the vision of His darkness. This is the mystical
moment, the "dark night of the soul" that compels the
mystic to brush against the abyss which separates finitude from infinity.
    The ram in the Akedah story represents this void, or

the modality of *ayin*. It is the ram which conjoins Abraham (love) with Isaac (fear) through its own self-sacrifice/self-annihilation. But the ram also represents the mode of transformation, for it is through the liminality of nothingness—which is violent, annihilative, and fearful—that the mystic can transform himself. In the mystical context, the ontic assault takes on redemptive properties: as being collides with nonbeing (*ayin*), it produces *new* being. This conception of *unio mystica* is not one of true merger. For the Maggid, the abyss which separates God from man cannot be crossed. Though the mystic is the vessel in which the divine spirit may dwell, he does not *become* that spirit. The abyss—*ayin*—is not equated with God Himself, but instead with His first emanation, or "thought," and a brush with it is force enough to transform the mystic into an utterly different person.

The Maggid utilizes this same paradigm to discuss the transformation of consciousness:

> "Come, my beloved, let us go forth into the field; let us lodge in the villages" [Song of Songs 7:12]. . . . This is the meaning of "Come, my beloved": the divine intellect (*ha-maskil*) says to the human intellect (*ha-sekhel*), "let us go forth into the field." This refers to the process of preparing [something] for consumption. The field produces grain, but the grain is not fit for consumption until it is brought to the village, where it is crushed; similarly, the human intellect is on a low level of conception, as if it is yet to be born from the womb of its mother. But later, it comes to the attribute of fear, which elevates it. This parallels the grain that is crushed in a village in order to "elevate" it—to bring it to the city [for consumption]. "Let us lodge in the villages" means to dwell in the divine attributes [sefirot], and [then] afterwards [it is written], "Let us get up early to

the vineyards" [Song of Songs 7:13]—so that we will
come to the great intellect (*sekhel gadol*).[6]

    This remarkable homily uses a verse from the Song
of Songs to explain the transformation of consciousness,
based on the model of the ontic assault. Grain harvested
from a field is not fit for consumption until it has first
been pulverized in the threshing houses of the village.
In the same way, human discursive thought is also on a
low level of primordial existence. It has not yet been
truly "born," like a seed in the soil or a fetus in the womb
of its mother. For grain, it is the act of threshing which
elevates its mode of existence to a higher order, so that
it may become flour to be brought to the city and transformed into bread. For discursive thought, it is the attribute of *fear* that elevates it to a higher existential state
and brings it to the level of divine thought. As the village
brings grain to the quality of *ayin*, so do the sefirot bring
the human mind to *unio mystica*.

    There are several key implications of this homily. At
the site of the "preparation" for metamorphosis—whether
physical or spiritual—great violence occurs. The procedure for a transformation of state is annihilative. For a
mode of existence to change into a new form, its prior
state must be destroyed, and this takes place as it passes
through *ayin*. Grain can only become food *after* it has
been crushed; human thought can only become divine
thought *after* the attribute of fear has "killed" its discursive state. Like the experience of birth pangs, the experience of fear is the pain that produces the mystic consciousness: it is the stage before and the preparation that
leads to *unio mystica*. The world of the sefirot—of which
fear is a part—is not an end in itself but the portal to the
"great intellect" which is wisdom, or the state of *ayin*.[7]

The transformation of man into "Nothing" is the bridge into the world of the spirit, where true spiritual processes and dynamics begin. Yet, as Schatz-Uffenheimer notes, "man's inability to obliterate his temporal being blocks the way to the breakthrough of the spirit"[8]; that is, the ontic void that separates the temporal from the eternal and the finite from the infinite cannot be crossed— only *encountered*. It remains an impenetrable fortress that prevents the merger of God and man. The Maggid writes that

> there is an attribute which connects the divine intel-
> lect with the human intellect, and this attribute is not
> comprehensible, for it is the attribute of *ayin*, which is
> the "hyle" [or the Platonic idea of eternal, formless
> matter]. This is illustrated through the parable of the
> egg from which a chick is born: there is a [certain] time
> when it is neither egg nor chick, and no man is able to
> grasp this [exact] moment, for it is then in the attribute
> of *ayin*.[9]

Every new birth must first pass through the noth-ingness of *ayin*, as when a chick emerges from an egg: for an instant—a moment that is beyond the ken of the human mind—it is "neither egg nor chick," but in a state of amorphous *hyle*.[10] As it relates to the transformation of consciousness, this psychological nothingness is a kind of rupture within the continuity of time, "by means of which man is plunged into the transnatural atmo-sphere; at the same time, it is a point of connection between the corporeal and the spiritual form of exist-ence."[11] The Maggid describes the transformation of the being of the egg into that of the chick (and that of the human intellect into the divine intellect) as a paradoxi-cal continuity within a "break." Because it occurs within

time and yet transcends it, no man can grasp this trans-
formative phenomenon, just as no man can pinpoint the
true instant of twilight, when the day dies and the night
is born.

According to this theory, there is no birth without
a death. When being collides with nonbeing, there is
violence, but in the wake of this assault comes new
being:

> No thing is able to change from [one] thing into some-
> thing else [without passing through *ayin*]. Before a
> chick can emerge from an egg, the being of the egg
> (that is, the chick's first form) must first be annihilated,
> and [only] afterwards is the new being [of the chick]
> able to emerge. All things must follow this process, and
> come to the level of *ayin* before they become some-
> thing else.[12]

Transformation of any kind is impossible without
the participation/mediation of *ayin*. Nothingness em-
braces every potentiality and is the necessary condition
for its actualization: the egg must be broken before the
chick can be born. At this point of *unio mystica*, world,
mind, and self disintegrate in *ayin* before their reemer-
gence into new forms. As Matt writes, "Every object,
every thought is revealed as an epiphany of *ayin*. Yet
ayin is not the goal in itself; it is the moment of transformation from being through nonbeing to new being."[13]
Annihilation is the sole process that engenders new life.
The purpose of *unio mystica* is not total extinction but
rather "the emergence of a new form, a more perfectly
human image of the divine."[14]

Since the phenomenon of *ayin* is connected to the
experience of fear, it becomes clear that no transforma-

tion can come about that does not involve this response. When the mystic encounters *ayin*, he is filled with fear, yet, as we saw in the parable about grain, it is just this experience (or rather its annihilative power) that transforms grain into bread and human thought into divine thought. The consequence of fear's ability to "kill" a previous form is its power to stimulate the "birth" of a new form, and in the mystical context this relates to the transformation of consciousness. The Maggid utilizes this dynamic in parables that explain the transformations which take place in the plant kingdom. He writes:

> [When] a man sows a single seed, it is known that it will not sprout to produce other seeds until its existence has [first] been annihilated. Then it is raised to its root, and can receive more than a single dimension of its existence. There in its root the seed itself becomes the source of many seeds, since it has adhered to its root. And this root of generative power seeks to spread [itself] always.[15]

Before a seed can grow into a plant, it must rot in the earth. As a result of its disintegration of form, the seed is able to take on a new form and, in consequence, produce even more seeds in its changed state.[16] The instant of annihilation, when the old form brushes (but does not merge) with the new form, is the point of *ayin*. It is in this mode that the seed is "raised" to its root, where, in an eternal moment, all ontic boundaries disappear; *ayin* is the death that generates life, the fullness of being that transcends being itself. This dialectic functions as a paradigm for the phenomenon of mystical encounter and is a further paradigm for God's relation to the world. The Maggid elaborates:

If the power of growth (*koah ha-tzomeiakh*) is always implanted in the earth, why does [the earth] not produce [food] even when nothing has been planted in it? The power of growth within the earth is without limit or boundary; it is like Eyn Sof in comparison to the emergence of a seed. When one sows a seed in the earth, and it adheres to the power of growth—which is its root and source—then the power of growth contracts its force and dwells in the seed. From the seed will emerge the [new] form, when both [the power of growth and the seed] reach "nought" (*efes*); after [this point] the new form will emerge from the two.[17]

The notion of emergence is inextricably tied to that of contraction. The Maggid compares the powers of nature with the being of God. Just as Eyn Sof (or He who is limitless) must contract His power and presence from the world in order for it to emerge and exist, so must the power of growth contract its force so that it can dwell in the seed and cause the emergence of the seed's new form. At the moment of "naught," or *ayin*, the seed collides with the power of growth and loses its identity. It is only *after* this ontic collision that the emergence of the seed's new form becomes possible. The point of decay is the point of fear; it is in this eternal instant that *ayin* "kills" the old form while simultaneously giving "birth" to the new one.

The Maggid applies this model to all transformations: "Every thing in the world, when it is brought to its root, is able to effect a transformation from what it once was [to what it will become]."[18] Similarly, when a man contracts himself and reaches his root (*ayin*), he passes through the abyss that separates old being from new being, like the butterfly which emerges from its tattered

cocoon. It is this dialectic that captures the psychic transformation which follows a brush with the void, or *unio
mystica*. As a paradox, this fearful/ecstatic moment fuses
the annihilative element with the generative one. Tillich
interprets these powers as the two aspects of the divine
presence, *mysterium tremendum* and *mysterium fascin-
osum*: it is *unio mystica* which unites the experience of
the abyss (nonbeing) with the experience of the ground
(being).[19] In the paradox of *ayin*, the mystic seeks his
death, yet discovers his life.

Conclusion

For the vast majority of Jewish thinkers, both before and after the birth of hasidism, the fear of God remained an amorphous term. Rather than serving as a referent for a specific experience, it was generally used as a designation for the inner life as a whole: ethics, piety, and faith seemed to coalesce into a single totality. In many instances, the fear of God was used as a counterfoil to the study of Torah,[1] seemingly as a metaphor for spiritual (as opposed to intellectual) development. In the early hasidic period, however, religious fear takes on not only more importance but far more sophistication. Yaakov Yosef and the Maggid are among the first, and possibly the best, exemplars of this innovation in Jewish thought.

As we have shown, it is through a phenomenological lens that these hasidic masters explore the notion of *yirah*. Yet Yaakov Yosef and the Maggid represent, even at this seminal stage of the movement, very different and characteristic approaches to the issues of Jewish spirituality. Their treatment of the fear of God makes this distinction clear. In Yaakov Yosef's system, the presence of the zaddik is critical to the interrelationship between human beings and God: it is the zaddik—in the role of intermediary—who effects the union of opposites (in this case, the union of the finite with the infinite). The fear of God is that attribute which leads to adhesion with God and, without the mediation of the zaddik, is inaccessible to the average man. This doctrine is elitist in that the zaddik, and he alone, is the necessary condition/element for communion with God; yet it is also populist, in that it grants to every man the *possibility* of that communion.

In the Maggid's thought, the zaddik loses his function as the intermediary between the hasid and God and is replaced by the phenomenological state of *ayin*. Because that element which unites the finite with infinity no longer takes the form of a specific personality, it becomes possible, in principle, for *any* individual to access the fear of God. It is this fear that leads to and punctuates the experience of *unio mystica*. With the elimination of intermediaries as prerequisites for this encounter, the Maggid constructs a theory of mystical consciousness and transformation that is founded on an immediacy so profound it can only be accurately described as a collision.

For Yaakov Yosef, the fear of God is the mechanism by which an individual is able to overcome all of his other, wordly fears. The negation of these external fears is what leads to the true purpose of the spiritual ascent: the redemption of the self. Yaakov Yosef posits a "mystical redemption of the individual here and now, i.e., redemption not *from* exile, but *in* exile,"[2] or the destruction of exile (which he associates with external fear) through its spiritualization. When the world of the mundane is aroused and elevated to the level of the supermundane, the end result is nothing less than salvation. It is fear which sets this dynamic into motion.

The Maggid presents a radically different position on the relationship between fear and the self. For him, the fear of God does not lead to the redemption of the self but rather to the very *annihilation* of the self. In the former case, self-consciousness is not only retained, but actually necessary. In the latter situation, self-consciousness is an obstruction to the hasid's elevation, and it is only as a result of its obliteration (through the experience of fear) that he can make room for the divine presence and facilitate the mystical encounter. The state of *ayin* that describes this phenomenon exists outside of time. With no notion of time and no concept of a self, the very idea of a "redemption" becomes irrelevant in his system. Instead, the Maggid discusses the *transformation* of the self and the fact that every new life requires a parallel death.

Yaakov Yosef and the Maggid also differ in their views on the achievability of the fear of God. From Yaakov Yosef's perspective, the fear of God is ultimately a dialectic of divine grace and human achievement. As we have shown, external fear is, in its essence, the manifestation of God's *hesed*/grace, and it is this manifestation of the divine influx that arouses man to the fear of God (internal fear). Yet this influx from the upper world is *itself* aroused by man's own activity in the lower world, producing the dialectic: that which man is given, he also brings about. The Maggid's position is much more straightforward. For him, the fear of God is the product of the mystic's own efforts or, to use his own word, "struggle." It is only after he actively contracts his

very sense of self that he creates the space in which
God may dwell, and it is this indwelling which produces
his experience of fear.

There are clear distinctions between Yaakov Yosef
and the Maggid on the issue of prayer. In keeping with
the teachings of his master, Yaakov Yosef advocates the
doctrine of *avodah be-gashmiyut* (the service of God
through corporeality). He argues that the soul must
always long for a return to its Root, yet, "lest its existence
become annihilated as a result of its yearning, it has been
encased in matter, so that it may perform material acts
such as eating, drinking, and the conduct of business."[3]
Corporeal worship, for Yaakov Yosef, saves man from
the dangers of an all-consuming spiritualism and an aban-
donment of the world of the here and now. Kierkegaard
claims that every passion, by definition, wills its own
destruction;[4] Yaakov Yosef utilizes the doctrine of *avodah be-gashmiyut* as a kind of "safety valve" which pre-
serves the soul from this self-destruction and makes
possible the idea of a personal redemption. One cannot
"strip" the garments except through the interaction *with*
them.

The Maggid offers a far more radicalized position
on the issue of prayer. Whereas Yaakov Yosef eschews
the notion of self-annihilation, the Maggid views it as
the primary goal of prayer. In a system where spiritual
transformation, as opposed to personal redemption, is
the final prize, self-awareness is treated as no more than
an impediment to the process as a whole. The Maggid
retains the concept of *avodah be-gashmiyut*, but holds
it as applicable only to the elite who have the ability to
transcend it. Unlike Yaakov Yosef, who supports peti-
tionary prayer as an acceptable form of worship, the
Maggid argues that only contemplative prayer is per-

missible for the mystic. Citing the verse, "Those who fear [God] have no lack" (Ps. 34:10), he claims that God-fearers lack nothing but the divine nothing (*ayin*) itself,[5] and thus have no need to petition for anything. It is through contemplative prayer—which the self-reflectiveness of petition necessarily hinders—that the mystic is able to vacate his sense of self and reach the point of *ayin*.

In the spiritual systems of both Yaakov Yosef and the Maggid, Moses and the story of the Exodus are used as metaphors. Yaakov Yosef views Moses as the paradigm for the zaddik, and it is he who embodies the fear of God. Moses functions as the intermediary between his people and God: as they fear him, so (through his mediation) will they come to fear God. Yaakov Yosef equates the bondage in Egypt with the oppressiveness of external, worldly fears. When one reaches the fear of God, however, all external fears (like the exile in Egypt) will be "negated," and the self (like the people of Israel) will be redeemed.

The Maggid similarly spiritualizes the Exodus imagery and treats the episode as a whole as a paradigm for *unio mystica*. Yet the Exodus is not, for him, a metaphor for the negation of worldly fears, but rather for the negation of existence *itself*. It is this negation that leads to self-annihilation: as the self is liberated from the *yesh*, it becomes possible for it to enter into the *ayin*—and "nothingness" is the place of Redemption, where the finite mind empties out and acquires a new capacity for infinity. The mystical consciousness is the absorption of this divine mind, and it is Moses who becomes the symbol of its actualization.

Yaakov Yosef and the Maggid are important exemplars of the hasidic mystical tradition, yet the differences between them are profound. Though both men view the fear of God as a necessary condition for the attainment of the revelatory encounter, it is only in the Maggid's thought that the mystical event is *itself* examined in depth. This event, for him, is a violent one; it is a collision of being with nonbeing, an irruption of the divine presence and consciousness within the soul and mind of man. Despite the fact that some tension exists on the issue of mystical "merger," the Maggid's position is generally clear: *unio mystica* cannot be truly described as a *merger* of man and God, but rather as a *brush* of one against the Other. When the mystic collides with the divine *ayin*, he comes into temporary contact, not with God (who is Eyn Sof and transcends all being), but with the *abyss* that forever separates the finite from infinity. The transformation which results from the violence and fear of this "ontic assault" is the product of a brush with that void, and not an actual union with God Himself.

It is clear that the Maggid recognizes the annihilative power of *unio mystica*. So does Yaakov Yosef, indirectly through his doctrine of mediation and directly through his statements on the potential dangers of the spiritual ascent. The difference is that the Maggid views its destructive force as the prerequisite to psychic transformation and, in this sense, fails to appreciate the inherent ambiguity in the *consequences* of the mystical event. For the Maggid, the fact that *unio mystica* shocks, disorients, and shatters the cognitive and psychic structures of the mystic somehow seems to "organically" correct itself: it is merely the portal through which he must pass on his way to transformation. The brush with the void does not destroy the mystic's mind nor cripple his psychological powers.

This position is problematic. It is not reasonable to suggest or imply that every individual will respond to the divine encounter in the same way. Take, for instance, the tale, viewed by many commentators as a parable for the mystical experience, of the four men who enter *Pardes* (BT Hagigah 14b). Only one of them, R. Akiva, survives the experience with all of his faculties intact. Ben Azzai dies, Ben Zoma goes insane, and Aher becomes a heretic. Some mystics will return from a collision with *ayin* as new beings; some will not return at all. Some mystics who experience the violence of this event will be able to overcome its more dangerous effects; some will be forever damaged. The point is that, in opposition to the Maggid's claim, there is no *necessary* consequence of *unio mystica*. If a brush with the void is a dialectic of rupture—the irruption (of God) and the disruption (of man)—then there is no way to escape its violence, its uncertainty, and its terror. With the proper attitude, however, with the *fear* of God, the mystic may afford himself at least some modicum of protection.

Notes

INTRODUCTION

1. See Søren Kierkegaard, *Fear and Trembling* (Princeton, NJ: Princeton University Press, 1983), pp. 15–23. Kierkegaard interprets God's command as a "teleological suspension of the ethical," and Abraham's response as one of "infinite resignation." What is being tested, argues Kierkegaard, is not the patriarch's moral rectitude, but his faith and obedience.

2. Louis Jacobs, *A Jewish Theology* (New York: Behrman House, 1973), p. 174.

3. See *Hovot ha-Levavot* (Jerusalem: Feldheim, 1962), vol. 2, chapter 10.

4. *Mishneh Torah* (Jerusalem, 1984), *Sefer ha-Madah,* pp. 99–100 and 650–652.

5. *Sefer ha-Ikkarim* (Philadelphia: Jewish Publication Society, 1946), vol. 3, chaps. 31–33, pp. 291–304.

6. See *Otzar Sefer Hasidim* (Jerusalem, 1992), pp. 162–164.

7. *Reshit Hokhmah* (Jerusalem: Or ha-Musar, 1984), vol. 1, *Sha'ar ha-Yirah*.

8. *Netivot Olam* (B'nei B'rak, 1980), vol. 2, pp. 20–37.

9. See Louis Jacobs, *Hasidic Prayer* (Washington, D.C.: B'nai B'rith, 1993), Introduction, p. xxiii.

PART 1

1. The whole question of whether hasidism represents a religious innovation or is part of a continuous flow is still a matter of scholarly debate. See Bezalel Safran, ed., *Hasidism: Continuity or Innovation?* (Cambridge, Mass.: Harvard University Press, 1988), and Scholem's final lecture in *Major Trends in Jewish Mysticism* (New York: Schocken, 1961).

CHAPTER 1

1. See Samuel Dresner, *The Zaddik* (London: Abelard-Schuman, 1960), p. 124, for this reference. It is the zaddik, says Dresner, who "brings heaven to earth and raises earth to heaven." The Maggid replaces the zaddik with the notion of *ayin*, or nothingness, as his mediating force between two opposites.

2. Arthur Green, "Typologies of Leadership and the Hasidic Zaddiq," in *Jewish Spirituality: From the Sixteenth-Century Revival to the Present* (New York: Crossroad, 1989), p. 128.

3. See Dresner, *The Zaddik*, pp. 247–248, where he quotes from the introduction: "I have come now with the help of the Creator to explain how it is that not one

of the 613 commandments lacks meaning for any man, wherever he may be. . . ."

4. Deuteronomy 10:20.

5. *Toledot Yaakov Yosef* (Jerusalem, 1973), vol. 2, p. 626.

6. Green, *Jewish Spirituality*, p. 149: ". . . the emerging Hasidic leader is in fact regularly referred to as *talmid hakham*, the *true* scholar/sage as distinct from those who had let this mantle become soiled."

7. *Toledot*, vol. 2, p. 629a.

8. Ibid.

9. Another term used to express this idea of the zaddik as medium is *emtza'i*. See *Zafnat Paneah* (Brooklyn, 1991), pp. 182b and 184b.

10. At the end of this homily he writes: ". . .the words of both [camps] are the words of the living God, and both are necessary for the thinker who wants to know the way [to make] the light dwell [upon him]." See *Toledot*, vol. 2, p. 629a.

11. Ibid., vol. 1, p. 155b.

12. Ibid.

13. Exodus 33:20.

14. *Zafnat Paneah*, p. 181b.

15. Ibid.

16. Ibid., p. 230a. Yaakov Yosef goes on here to compare the zaddik to a temple, both of which should inspire fear in us.

17. *Mekhilta, loc. cit.*

18. *Toledot*, vol. 2, p. 630a.

19. A pun on the words *atzmot* (bones) and *atzmut* (essence).

20. See *Zafnat Paneah*, p. 182b.

21. Ibid., p. 184.

CHAPTER 2

1. The combination of fear and love of God as
religious attributes goes back as far as the Talmud (BT
Sotah 31a) but is first systematically developed in medieval Jewish literature.
2. *Toledot*, vol. 2, p. 628a.
3. *Zafnat Paneah*, p. 180.
4. The appellation of "God-fearer" is pre-rabbinic.
Cf. Gen. 22:12 for one of the more famous examples.
5. *Mishneh Torah* (Jerusalem, 1984), pp. 99–100.
6. See *Toledot*, vol. 2, p. 630b. He seems to para-
phrase Maimonides here.
7. Ibid.
8. Ibid., pp. 630b–631a.
9. See Moshe Idel, *Kabbalah: New Perspectives*
(New Haven, Conn.: Yale University Press, 1988), p. 107.
10. This move is a radical reversal of the kabbalistic
association of fear with the *left* side of the sefirot.
11. See *Ben Porat Yosef* (New York, 1954), p. 43a.
12. Ibid.
13. A thinker more or less contemporaneous with
Yaakov Yosef who also elevates the notion of sin to
such a spiritual level is Luzzatto. Cf. Moshe Chayim
Luzzatto, *The Path of the Just* (Jerusalem: Feldheim,
1990), pp. 311–321.
14. See Gershom G. Scholem, *Major Trends in Jewish Mysticism* (New York: Schocken, 1961), pp. 340–341.
He writes that, in hasidism, "the secrets of the divine
realm are presented in the guise of mystical psychology. It is by descending into the depths of one's own
self that man wanders through all the dimensions of the
world."

CHAPTER 3

1. *Ben Porat Yosef*, p. 99a.

2. Jacob Immanuel Schochet, *Mystical Concepts in Chassidism* (Brooklyn: Kehilot, 1979), p. 81.

3. Louis Jacobs, *A Jewish Theology* (New York: Behrman House, 1973), p. 179.

4. *Ben Porat Yosef*, p. 86b. The kabbalah traditionally associates Abraham with the attribute of love, Isaac with the attribute of fear, and Jacob with a fusion of the two.

5. See Joseph Weiss, *Studies in Eastern European Jewish Mysticism* (New York: Oxford, 1985), p. 105. This text occurs in his article titled "The Kavvanoth of Prayer in Early Hasidism."

6. Scholem, p. 269.

7. *Zafnat Paneah*, pp. 180b-181a.

8. This is the one passage in our study of Yaakov Yosef that seems to betray any kind of quietistic tendency in his brand of mysticism. The idea of *heder ha-metzi'ut* comes very close to the notion of *bitul memetzi'ut*, which infuses much of the Maggid's work.

9. This view of fear serves as the answer to a philosophical problem: "Since the Holy One, blessed be He, is called awesome (*norah*), why is it necessary for the Torah to establish a commandment to fear Him?" Should it not simply be self-evident? Yaakov Yosef claims that it is not the lower form of fear to which the Torah refers (and which naturally inheres in all creatures), but its higher manifestation. It is this internal fear which must be commanded, and it is thus "appropriate that man should possess this additional level [at least *in potentia*]" (*Zafnat Paneah*, p. 181a). The Torah commands fear—

and only fear—as the critical requirement for covenantal living; surely that fear must transcend the simple fears of the beasts of the field.

CHAPTER 4

1. See *Toledot*, vol. 2, p. 635a.

2. This is a reference to a verse from Isaiah: "And he shall be the stability of thy times, a store of salvation, wisdom and knowledge; the fear of the Lord is his treasure" (Is. 33:6).

3. *Toledot*, vol. 2, p. 635b.

4. Ibid., p. 636a.

5. Ibid., p. 628b.

6. Ibid.

7. Ibid., p. 630b.

8. See *Ben Porat Yosef*, p. 98b: "When a man understands that [external fears] are God's grace . . . and [meant] to arouse him [to internal fear], his fear transforms into love. When he accepts this in love, he negates the external fears."

9. See *Mishneh Torah*, pp. 99–100.

10. *Toledot*, vol. 2, pp. 631b-632a.

11. Ibid., p. 630b.

12. *Zafnat Paneah*, p. 181a, and also *Ben Porat Yosef*, p. 99a.

13. See Ex. 7:16, 7:26, 8:16, 9:1, and many other verses.

14. *Zafnat Paneah*, p. 182b.

15. Ibid.

16. Ibid., p. 79a.

PART 2

1. See Simon Dubnow, "The Maggid of Miedzyr-zecz, His Associates, and the Center in Volhynia (1760–1772)," in *Essential Papers on Hasidism: Origins to Present* (New York: New York University, 1991), pp. 62–63.

CHAPTER 1

1. *Maggid Devarav le-Yaakov* (Jerusalem, 1990), p. 292.
2. Ibid., pp. 230–231.
3. Scholem, *Major Trends*, pp. 260–261. See section four in his seventh lecture, "Isaac Luria and His School," for an excellent overview of the Lurianic conception of *tzimtzum*.
4. *Maggid Devarav le-Yaakov*, p. 24.
5. See *Likutim Yekarim* (Jerusalem, 1974), pp. 105b-106a.
6. Scholem, *Major Trends*, p. 263.
7. *Or ha-Emet* (Brooklyn, 1960), p. 113, and *Or Torah* (Lublin, 1910), p. 60b.
8. As opposed to the views of Scholem and, more recently, Steven Katz, this text clearly challenges the claim that all Jewish mystical testimonies conform to a "dualistic" notion of *unio mystica*, where the mystic and God remain distinct and separate entities. In this passage, the Maggid describes an experience of merger and absorption *into* God which reveals a tension on this issue within his own thought.
9. *Or ha-Emet*, p. 92.

10. *Likutim Yekarim*, p. 106a.

11. *Shemuah Tovah* (Warsaw, 1938), p. 73b.

12. See Rivka Schatz-Uffenheimer, *Hasidism as Mysticism: Quietistic Elements in Eighteenth Century Hasidic Thought* (Princeton, N.J.: Princeton University Press, 1993), p. 171.

13. *Or ha-Emet*, p. 40.

14. *Maggid Devarav le-Yaakov*, p. 10.

15. Schatz-Uffenheimer, *Hasidism as Mysticism*, p. 207.

16. See the introduction to the Zohar and *Tikkuney Zohar*, ch. 6; the comment refers to the divine mind, not the human mind.

17. *Maggid Devarav le-Yaakov*, pp. 11–12.

18. Schatz-Uffenheimer, *Hasidism as Mysticism*, p. 208.

19. *Maggid Devarav le-Yaakov*, p. 186.

CHAPTER 2

1. This passage occurs in at least two of the Maggid's sources: *Or ha-Emet*, p. 140, and *Or Torah*, pp. 77b-78a.

2. This, and the following passage, appear with slight variations in *Or Torah*, p. 59b, and *Likutim Yekarim*, p. 75.

3. Ibid.

4. *Or ha-Emet*, p. 71.

5. Ibid., pp. 72–73. The Zohar itself mentions three types of fear, but "in two of them there is no proper principle." The only authentic fear is "when a man fears his Master because He is the great Ruler, the basic principle and root of all worlds, compared with whom noth-

ing is of any worth." The Maggid connects this with the fear of shame.

6. In this passage the Maggid clearly views the God-fearer as the spiritual superior of the zaddik. Bearing in mind his lack of emphasis on the role of the zaddik, could this be a polemic against the Maggid's cultural context, in which the zaddik was beginning to be viewed, and treated, as a member of some kind of religious royal class?

7. *Shemuah Tovah*, p. 26.

8. *Or Torah*, p. 59b, and *Likutim Yekarim*, p. 75.

9. *Shemuah Tovah*, p. 73b.

10. Ibid., p. 74a.

11. *Maggid Devarav le-Yaakov*, p. 71.

12. *Or ha-Emet*, p. 2.

13. *Or Torah*, p. 60a.

14. Ibid., p. 81.

15. See *Maggid Devarav le-Yaakov*, p. 188: "The *Shekhinah* is called Jerusalem (*Yerushalayim*), or *yirah shalem*, since from it come all the [other] fears. They all fell at the Breaking [of the Vessels], and thus are not whole (*shalem*); but the fear of God is whole fear (*yirah shelemah*)."

16. Unlike the love of God, which the Maggid views as a gift of divine grace, the fear of God is seen as within man's power to achieve, and thus its attainment as his spiritual responsibility. See *Likutim Yekarim*, p. 42b, *Or Torah*, p. 60a, and *Or ha-Emet*, p. 72.

CHAPTER 3

1. *Maggid Devarav le-Yaakov*, p. 36.

2. Ibid.

3. Ibid., p. 68. This verse from Job is commonly

used among Jewish mystics as a proof text by which to
associate wisdom with nothingness.

    4. *Shemuah Tovah*, p. 29a.

    5. *Maggid Devarav le-Yaakov*, p. 186.

    6. Ibid., p. 229. It is interesting how Moses serves
as the paradigm for the spiritual "superman" in each
generation of Jewish thinkers. For the rabbis, he is *Moshe
Rabbenu*; for Maimonides, he is the philosopher par
excellence; for the hasidim, he becomes the quintes-
sential mystic.

    7. Daniel Matt, "*Ayin*: the Concept of Nothingness
in Jewish Mysticism," in *The Problem of Pure Consciousness: Mysticism and Philosophy* (New York: Oxford
University Press, 1990), p. 140.

    8. *Shemuah Tovah*, p. 29a.

    9. Ibid.

    10. Schatz-Uffenheimer, *Hasidism as Mysticism*,
p. 73.

    11. *Maggid Devarav le-Yaakov*, pp. 97–98.

    12. Ibid., pp. 38–39.

    13. See Idel, *Kabbalah: New Perspectives*, p. 66.

    14. Schatz-Uffenheimer, *Hasidism as Mysticism*,
p. 176.

    15. *Or ha-Emet*, pp. 4–5.

    16. *Likutim Yekarim*, p. 7a.

    17. See Paul Tillich, *Systematic Theology: Volume
One* (Chicago: University of Chicago Press, 1951), p. 112.

    18. *Likutim Yekarim*, p. 63a.

    19. Schatz-Uffenheimer, *Hasidism as Mysticism*,
p. 185.

    20. See Søren Kierkegaard, *Fear and Trembling*
(Princeton, N.J.: Princeton University Press, 1983), pp. 39–
40.

    21. The image of God as a "consuming fire" can

be found throughout the Bible. See Deu. 4:24 and 9:3, Is. 29:6 and 33:14, and Joel 2:5.

22. *Or ha-Emet*, p. 186.

23. See Idel, *Kabbalah: New Perspectives*, pp. 70–73.

24. *Or Torah*, p. 61a. The phrase *matei ve'lo matei* appears in the Zohar and is used in relation to the radicality of God's transcendence: the highest aspects of God simply cannot be expressed. See Bereshit I: 15a, 16b, and 65a.

25. The Maggid argues that though no mystical phenomenon (including the fear of God) is constant, each leaves a "trace" (*roshem*) after it has passed. In the case of fear, that trace is humility. See *Or ha-Emet*, p. 63.

26. Schatz-Uffenheimer, *Hasidism as Mysticism*, p. 179.

27. *Or ha-Emet*, pp. 32–33.

28. *Maggid Devarav le-Yaakov*, p. 98.

29. *Shemuah Tovah*, pp. 79b-80a.

30. Schatz-Uffenheimer, *Hasidism as Mysticism*, p. 172.

31. *Shemuah Tovah*, p. 70.

32. Ibid., p. 49.

CHAPTER 4

1. *Maggid Devarav le-Yaakov*, p. 134.

2. This parallels Yaakov Yosef's utilization of the zaddik as the medium between the masses and God.

3. *Maggid Devarav le-Yaakov*, pp. 253–254.

4. See Pirkei Avot 5:6, which lists the ten things that were created during the transition (dusk) between the six days of creation and the first Sabbath.

5. *Maggid Devarav le-Yaakov*, pp. 19–20.

6. Ibid., pp. 35–37.

7. See Matt, *The Problem of Pure Consciousness*, p. 135: "The sefirot are stages of contemplative ascent. . . . At the ultimate stage [of *hokhmah/ayin*] . . . conceptual thought, with all its distinctions and connections, dissolves."

8. Schatz-Uffenheimer, *Hasidism as Mysticism*, p. 174.

9. *Maggid Devarav le-Yaakov*, pp. 83–84 and *Or ha-Emet*, pp. 18–19.

10. Ibid. Schatz-Uffenheimer comments that, in the kabbalah, *hyle* (as primordial matter) was identified with the sefirah of *hokhmah*. In the Maggid's thought, where *hokhmah* is associated with *ayin*, the symbolism of *hyle* remains, but its meaning changes: the foundation of existence (*hyle*) becomes "the dialectical point of transformation of one thing into another."

11. Schatz-Uffenheimer, *Hasidism as Mysticism*, p. 173.

12. *Maggid Devarav le-Yaakov*, p. 49. The Maggid notes here that even miracles, such as Sarah's giving birth in her old age, must first reach the point of nothingness before they can occur. For similar discussions, see p. 91 and p. 277.

13. Matt, *The Problem of Pure Consciousness*, pp. 144–145.

14. Ibid., p. 145.

15. *Maggid Devarav le-Yaakov*, p. 209.

16. Cf. John 12:24: "Unless a grain of wheat falls into the earth and dies, it remains alone; but if it dies, it bears much fruit." There are many other examples of the seed metaphor for spiritual metamorphosis. See Matt, *The Problem of Pure Consciousness*, p. 158, n. 130.

17. *Maggid Devarav le-Yaakov*, p. 210.

18. Ibid., p. 134.

19. Paul Tillich, *Systematic Theology*, p. 113. See also Kierkegaard's discussion on God as the absolute paradox in *Philosophical Fragments* (Princeton, N.J.: Princeton University Press, 1985), part III and appendix. As a negative theologian, Kierkegaard claims that seeking to "think" the unknown leads first to what he calls "offense," and then later to faith.

CONCLUSION

1. This juxtaposition becomes especially pronounced in much of the later Musar literature.

2. See Gershom Scholem, *The Messianic Idea in Judaism and Other Essays on Jewish Spirituality* (New York: Schocken, 1971), p. 195.

3. See *Toledot*, vol. 1, p. 312a.

4. Kierkegaard, *Philosophical Fragments*, p. 37.

5. *Or Torah*, p. 78a.

Bibliography

I. HASIDIC SOURCES

Dov Baer of Mezeritch. *Likutim Yekarim*. Jerusalem, 1974.

———. *Maggid Devarav le-Yaakov*. Critical edition, with introduction, commentary, notes, and index by Rivka Schatz-Uffenheimer. Jerusalem: the Magnes Press, 1990.

———. *Or ha-Emet*. Brooklyn, 1960.

———. *Or Torah*. Lublin, 1910.

———. *Shemuah Tovah*. Warsaw, 1938.

Nahman of Tcherin. *Derekh Hasidim*. Lemberg, 1876.

———. *Leshon Hasidim*. Lemberg, 1876.

Yaakov Yosef of Polonnoye. *Ben Porat Yosef*. New York, 1954.

———. *Ketonet Passim*. Ed. G. Nigal. Jerusalem, 1985.

———. *Toledot Yaakov Yosef*, 2 vol., Jerusalem, 1973.

———. *Zafnat Paneah*. Brooklyn, 1991.

II. OTHER PRIMARY SOURCES

Albo, Joseph. *Sefer ha-Ikkarim*. Philadelphia, 1946.
Eleazar of Worms. *Sefer ha-Rokeah*. Jerusalem, n.d.
Judah the Hasid. *Sefer Hasidim*. Jerusalem, 1957.
Loew, Judah. *Netivot Olam*. B'nei B'rak, 1980.
Luzzatto, Moshe. *Mesillat Yesharim*. Jerusalem, 1966.
Pakuda, Bakhya ibn. *Hovot ha-Levavvot*. Jerusalem, 1962.
Vidas, Elijah de. *Reshit Hokhmah*. Jerusalem, 1984.

III. SECONDARY LITERATURE

Bergman, Shmuel Hugo. *Dialogical Philosophy from
    Kierkegaard to Buber*. Trans. Arnold A. Gerstein.
    Albany, New York: State University of New York
    Press, 1991.
Bloch, Joshua. "A Legendary Edition of the *Toledot Jacob
    Joseph* by Jacob Joseph ha-Kohen of Polonnoye."
    The Jewish Quarterly Review 31 (1940): 245–251.
Buber, Martin. *Hasidism and Modern* Man. Atlantic High-
    lands, New Jersey: Humanities Press International,
    1958.
———. *I and Thou*. New York: Charles Scribner's Sons,
    1970.
———. *The Origin and Meaning of Hasidism*. Atlantic
    Highlands, New Jersey: Humanities Press Interna-
    tional, 1960.
Dresner, Samuel H. *The Zaddik*. London: Abelard-
    Schuman, 1960.
Dubnow, Simon. "The Maggid of Miedzyrzecz, His As-
    sociates, and the Center in Volhynia (1760–1772)."
    Essential Papers on Hasidism: Origins to Present. Ed.
    Gershon David Hundert. New York: New York Uni-
    versity Press, 1991.

Etkes, Immanuel. *Rabbi Israel Salanter and the Mussar Movement: Seeking the Torah of Truth.* Philadelphia: The Jewish Publication Society, 1993.

Faierstein, Morris M. "Hasidism—the Last Decade in Research." *Modern Judaism* 11: 111–124.

Green, Arthur. *Tormented Master: The Life and Spiritual Quest of Rabbi Nahman of Bratslav.* Woodstock, Vermont: Jewish Lights Publishing, 1992.

————."Typologies of Leadership and the Hasidic Zaddiq." *Jewish Spirituality: From the Sixteenth-Century Revival to the Present.* Ed. Arthur Green. New York: Crossroad, 1989.

Heschel, Abraham J. *The Circle of the Baal Shem Tov: Studies in Hasidism.* Chicago: The University of Chicago Press, 1985.

————.*God in Search of Man: A Philosophy of Judaism.* New York: Farrar, Straus and Giroux, 1955.

Idel, Moshe. *Kabbalah: New Perspectives.* New Haven, Connecticut: Yale University Press, 1988.

Jacobs, Louis. *Hasidic Prayer.* London: The Littman Library of Jewish Civilization, 1993.

————. *A Jewish Theology.* New York: Behrman House, 1973.

James, William. *The Varieties of Religious Experience.* New York: Penguin Books, 1985.

Katz, Steven T. "Language, Epistemology, and Mysticism." *Mysticism and Philosophical Analysis.* Ed. Steven T. Katz. New York: Oxford University Press, 1978.

Kierkegaard, Søren. *Fear and Trembling.* Trans. Edward V. Hong and Edna H. Hong. Princeton, New Jersey: Princeton University Press, 1983.

————. *Philosophical Fragments.* Trans. Edward V. Hong and Edna H. Hong. Princeton, New Jersey: Princeton University Press, 1985.

Matt, Daniel C. "*Ayin*: The Concept of Nothingness in Jewish Mysticism." *The Problem of Pure Consciousness*. New York: Oxford University Press, 1990.

Otto, Rudolf. *The Idea of the Holy*. Trans. J. W. Harvey. New York: Oxford University Press, 1958.

Proudfoot, Wayne. *Religious Experience*. Berkeley, California: University of California Press, 1985.

Safran, Bezalel. "Maharal and Early Hasidim." *Hasidism: Continuity or Innovation?* Ed. Bezalel Safran. Cambridge, Massachusetts: Harvard University Press, 1988.

Schatz-Uffenheimer, Rivka. "Contemplative Prayer in Hasidism." *Studies in Mysticism and Religion*. Jerusalem: the Magnes Press, 1967.

————. *Hasidism as Mysticism: Quietistic Elements in Eighteenth Century Hasidic Thought*. Princeton, New Jersey: Princeton University Press, 1993.

Schleiermacher, Friedrich. *On Religion: Speeches to Its Cultured Despisers*. New York: Harper and Row, 1958.

Schochet, Jacob Immanuel. *Mystical Concepts in Chassidism: An Introduction to Kabbalistic Concepts and Doctrines*. Brooklyn: Kehot Publication Society, 1979.

Scholem, Gershom. *Major Trends in Jewish Mysticism*. New York: Schocken Books, 1971.

————. *The Messianic Idea in Judaism and Other Essays on Jewish Spirituality*. New York: Schocken Books, 1971.

————. *On the Kabbalah and Its Symbolism*. New York: Schocken Books, 1965.

Sherwin, Byron L. "Fear of God." *Contemporary Jewish Religious Thought*. Ed. Arthur A. Cohen and Paul Mendes-Flohr. New York: Charles Scribner's Sons, 1987.

Stace, W. T. *Mysticism and Philosophy.* Los Angeles: Jeremy P. Tarcher, 1960.

Tillich, Paul. *Systematic Theology.* Vol. 1. Chicago: The University of Chicago Press, 1951.

Tracy, David. *The Analogical Imagination: Christian Theology and the Culture of Pluralism.* New York: Crossroad, 1989.

Underhill, Evelyn. *Mysticism.* New York: Doubleday, 1990.

Weiss, Joseph. *Studies in Eastern European Jewish Mysticism.* New York: Oxford University Press, 1985.

Index

145

About the Author

Niles E. Goldstein is the assistant rabbi at Temple Israel in New Rochelle, New York. He holds a degree in philosophy from the University of Pennsylvania, and was ordained by the Hebrew Union College-Jewish Institute of Religion (New York), where he later served as an adjunct faculty member in the department of Philosophy/Theology. Rabbi Goldstein is the coauthor of *Judaism and Spiritual Ethics,* and has written and lectured on Jewish mysticism and spirituality. He is also a poet, and is currently writing a book on the soul. He lives in Brooklyn, New York.